The Beginners Guide to Living Trusts

Build a Living Trust, Skip Probate, and Secure Your Family's Future

Abbix Publishing Company

ABBIX PUBLISHING COMPANY
PUBLISHING THE EXTRAORDINARY

Abbix Publishing Company

Contents

Introduction

I remember sitting at my grandmother's kitchen table, surrounded by stacks of documents. She was meticulously explaining her living trust to me, and at the time, it felt like I was listening to a foreign language. The legal jargon flew over my head, yet my grandmother spoke with such calm assurance that I couldn't help but feel captivated. It was during these conversations that a seed was planted—one that would later shape my understanding of estate planning in profound ways. Little did I know that the wisdom she shared with me would prove invaluable not just for my own life, but also as guidance for others navigating similar paths.

We often don't think about estate planning until it's thrust upon us by necessity. But here's the truth: estate planning isn't just reserved for the wealthy or those approaching their twilight years. It's an important aspect of financial management that affects everyone, regardless of their bank balance. Whether you're an individual eyeing the horizon to ensure your loved ones are cared for, or someone with limited resources searching for affordable peace of mind, having a plan is empowering. Estate planning guarantees that your wishes are honored and your loved ones protected, eliminating guesswork and potential family disputes down the line. As one insightful planner once told me, "A well-structured estate plan is like a roadmap—helping your family navigate through the complexities of life after you're gone." It's a gift that keeps giving, ensuring that your legacy is exactly what you envisioned.

In this guide, we'll understand the complexities surrounding living trusts and estate planning. We'll begin with the basics, offering straightforward definitions that will make it easier to understand the common terminology. You'll discover practical steps to set up your own living trust, exploring how they can serve as effective tools for avoiding probate and safeguarding your heirs from unnecessary stress. We'll also tackle the common misconceptions that can deter people from taking action, providing simple strategies that suit different financial situations. By the end of the book, you'll be equipped to create an estate plan that aligns with your values and circumstances, no matter where you stand financially.

Let me ask you this: Have you ever given thought to what would happen to your assets if something unexpected were to occur? Or who would manage your affairs if you became incapacitated? These questions might seem daunting, or perhaps even easy to ignore when you're caught up in the whirlwind of daily life. However, they are critical to address now, rather than waiting until it's too late to make informed decisions. This book aims to encourage you to pause, reflect, and take action. Think of it as a gentle nudge towards securing your future and the future of those you cherish most.

This doesn't require extensive legal knowledge or deep pockets. It simply calls for a willingness to begin. Through relatable experiences, simplified explanations, and a relaxed conversational tone, this book is designed to meet you where you are and guide you forward step by step. You'll find insights tailored for individuals starting their estate planning from scratch, as well as for those seeking affordable solutions without needing extensive legal assistance. Along the way, I'll share personal anecdotes and the lessons learned from my own experiences, illustrating just how impactful these decisions can be.

So, let's understand the world of estate planning together. I hope that by the end of this book, you'll feel empowered to create an estate plan that reflects your intentions, secures your assets, and provides clarity and security for the ones you love. Let's embark on this journey toward peace of mind, knowing that each step you take will pave the way for a smoother, more assured future.

Chapter 1: Living Trusts: A Comprehensive Overview

Think of booking a vacation, one that you've meticulously saved for and dreamed about. You've chosen the perfect destination, packed your bags with anticipation, but upon arrival, you discover no reservation was ever made. The journey to get there, filled with excitement, suddenly turns into frustration and confusion as you scramble to figure things out on the spot. This is what estate planning can feel like without a proper structure in place, filled with the best intentions, yet potentially chaotic and burdensome when it matters most.

Many people find themselves in this position when they believe their simple 'will' covers everything or assume their assets will naturally transfer to loved ones without difficulty. They don't realize the complexities involved until it's too late, when family members face long waits, legal fees, and public scrutiny over personal matters. In this chapter, we'll understand how living trusts serve as an essential tool, offering control, clarity, and peace, ensuring your life's work doesn't become an unpredictable journey for those you care about.

Understanding Living Trusts

Think of a living trust as a practical toolbox created while you're alive, ready to manage and pass on your belongings seamlessly after you're gone, all while ensuring your directions are followed to the letter. It's not just about having control over who gets what, but also making sure these decisions align with your personal wishes and minimize hassles for your loved ones later.

Relationships shape every trust; there's the grantor (that's you, the creator), trustees (the individuals who manage the trust), and beneficiaries (those who benefit from it). Clarity in these roles is vital. As a grantor, choosing a reliable trustee is important since tasks often include asset management and distribution according to your wishes.

Legal Document

At its heart, a living trust is a legal construct, a kind of container into which you can place your assets like property, stocks, or savings. You, as the grantor, not only set it up, but you may also manage it yourself while you're alive. This offers a unique blend of control and security, ensuring that your assets are handled just as you envision.

Then comes flexibility. Living trusts can be morphed to meet your needs. Consider a revocable living trust, which means you can tweak or entirely dismantle it as life throws different situations at you. Perhaps you want to add a grandchild as a beneficiary or decide later to sell a piece of property—such trusts allow these changes with ease. This fluidity is incredibly beneficial, letting you keep your estate planning fresh and relevant as circumstances evolve.

Why bother with a living trust at all? The primary draw is in its simplicity and effectiveness in estate management. Unlike probate, which is the court-driven process a will undergoes after one's death, a living trust bypasses this process. That means your assets move directly to your chosen beneficiaries without court intervention, saving time, money, and shielding any squabbles from public scrutiny.

Types of Living Trusts

Living trusts come in two main forms—revocable and irrevocable—each catering to different needs and goals. A revocable trust provides flexibility, allowing you to retain control over your assets. You can modify or dissolve it as your circumstances or preferences evolve, making it a convenient choice for those seeking adaptability in their estate planning.

Irrevocable trusts, however, require you to relinquish control once they are established. While these trusts are more rigid and cannot be easily changed, they offer significant advantages, such as protection from certain taxes and creditors. This makes them an attractive option for individuals prioritizing asset protection or tax efficiency.

Let's understand this in a more detailed way. A revocable trust offers flexibility for an evolving life. For instance, say you buy a vacation home later down the line. This addition can shape the trust's structure, whether you plan weekly getaways or eventually want beneficiaries to inherit that haven. The capacity to adapt is important, especially if new heirs emerge or relationships evolve.

Consider this example: You set up a revocable trust and assign your sister as trustee. Over time, your portfolio grows, and rules restrict her from using those resources wisely. Perhaps she can't sell a specific stock when market conditions shift. Because the trust is revocable, you refine it, defining more flexible asset management guidelines. This prevents unnecessary stress or arguments, ensuring a smoother process in your absence.

Irrevocable trusts serve a different purpose; although the rigidity sounds like a drawback, they hold distinct advantages like minimizing estate taxes and offering asset protection. Consider this: you're a small business owner aiming to safeguard parts of your net worth from potential creditors. An irrevocable trust diligently segregates those assets, offering peace of mind not typically found elsewhere. This setup carves out a financial space that's impervious to various pitfalls, ensuring certain parts of your estate remain untouched.

Choosing the right type of trust depends on the level of control you wish to maintain and the specific objectives you aim to achieve—whether it's tax savings, enhanced privacy, safeguarding assets, or a combination of these benefits. Each option serves its purpose, and understanding their distinctions will help align your choice with your long-term goals.

When considering modifications, remember that updating roles, particularly those of beneficiaries and trustees, is only straightforward with revocable trusts. This characteristic can prevent family conflicts, allowing you to incorporate life changes effortlessly, like adding a new spouse or recognizing a friend for enduring loyalty with tangible assets.

Understanding the key difference between living trusts and wills is essential for creating a complete estate plan. Living trusts provide more privacy, while wills involve a public probate process. Deciding between these options or using both depends on your specific needs and goals. Next, we'll understand how living trusts and wills can work together to support your estate planning strategy.

Differences and Advantages of Living Trusts Over Wills

Living trusts differ from wills in significant ways, offering unique advantages in estate planning.

Probate Process

One of the primary benefits is probate avoidance, which can save you time, money, and stress. When you have a will, your estate typically goes through a probate process. This procedure can be lengthy and costly, involving court fees and potentially long waiting periods before your heirs receive their inheritance. A living trust circumvents this process entirely, allowing for an immediate transfer of assets upon your demise, controlled by your chosen trustee.

Consider a scenario where an individual named Jane passes away with only a will in place. Her family might wait several months, dealing with court proceedings, hearings, and associated legal costs. In contrast, if Jane had set up a living trust, her assets could be distributed to her beneficiaries within weeks, preserving wealth and reducing administrative burdens. This distinction highlights the practical advantage of living trusts over traditional wills, showcasing how they enhance asset management and distribution efficiency.

Accessibility During Lifetime

Another key benefit of living trusts is their capacity to manage your assets during incapacity. Think of a situation where someone becomes mentally or physically unable to manage their affairs due to illness or an accident. A living trust can ensure that their financial life continues seamlessly without court intervention. The trustee you've named can immediately step in to manage your assets, pay bills, and handle other financial responsibilities. This readiness to act preserves your estate's integrity and ensures your affairs are in the hands of someone you trust.

Privacy Concerns

Living trusts offer privacy that wills simply cannot. When a will is probated, it becomes a matter of public record, meaning anyone can access information about your assets and who inherits them. For those valuing discretion, this openness can be concerning. In contrast, living trusts remain private documents, only disclosed to parties involved. This aspect brings peace of mind, knowing that details about your wealth and its distribution remain among those you choose.

Flexibility of Changes

Living trusts provide flexible asset distribution. With a will, assets are distributed in lump sums, which might not align with the needs or maturity of the heirs. A living trust allows you to set specific terms for the distribution of your assets. For example, you can stipulate that your children receive portions of their inheritance at different ages or life milestones, such as completing college or reaching a certain age. This structure secures prudent financial management and ensures your legacy is utilized in ways that align with your values and foresight.

Understanding the financial benefits of living trusts often leads to emotional reassurance. You can rest easy knowing your affairs won't become public knowledge, your estate will be managed even if you cannot, and your assets will be distributed according to your specifications. This level of control and privacy can alleviate a significant amount of worry, allowing you to focus on the present, knowing the future is well looked after.

These benefits make living trusts a valuable tool for those with limited financial resources. The ability to streamline asset management and stay out of court can free up funds that might otherwise be spent on legal fees and extended proceedings—money that could instead bolster the inheritance you leave behind.

Now that we've explored the numerous benefits of living trusts, the next logical step is to understand how they're structured. Understanding the basic components of a living trust provides further empowerment by simplifying how this effective estate planning tool functions.

Setting up a living trust involves a clear, structured process that we'll discuss next. We'll cover how to establish one, the roles within it, and how you can tailor it to fit your personal and financial goals. Knowing this empowers you to make informed decisions about your estate planning that align with both your practical needs and emotional desires, ensuring that your legacy supports the people you care about in meaningful ways.

Key Benefits of Living Trusts

In the world of estate planning, living trusts stand out for their ability to bypass the often lengthy and costly probate process, bringing both peace and efficiency to families navigating the aftermath of a loved one's passing. This distinction is more than just a fiscal or temporal benefit as it offers a smoother, less stressful transition, granting invaluable peace of mind. Rather than entangling family members in months of court proceedings, a living trust ensures that assets transfer seamlessly, often privately, delivering both time and emotional relief at a time when families need it most.

Management of Assets During Incapacity

Avoiding probate is just the beginning. A key advantage of living trusts lies in their design to effectively manage assets if you, the grantor, become incapacitated. If you ever find yourself incapacitated and unable to make financial decisions due to health issues, the absence of a trust could result in your financial matters being handled by the courts, adding unnecessary stress to an already challenging situation for you and your loved ones. Through a living trust, you maintain control by appointing a successor trustee, someone you trust, to handle your financial matters. Picture Joseph, a vibrant 60-year-old, who faced an unforeseen stroke. Because he had set up a living trust, his son, his chosen successor, stepped in immediately to manage his expenses and healthcare needs without a court's intervention, allowing Joseph to focus on his recovery while preserving family stability.

Control Over Asset Distribution

In addition to asset management during incapacitation, living trusts provide more nuanced control over how and when your beneficiaries receive their inheritance. Grantors can stipulate specific terms, perhaps you want your children to inherit when they turn 30, or maybe distribute funds gradually to ensure they have financial security over time. For example, consider a family with young children. They can clearly define how funds are to be distributed, ensuring their children receive enough for their education or living expenses as they grow, without the risk of young children or financially inexperienced family members mishandling their inheritance.

Prevent Disputes

Living trusts help prevent disputes by providing clarity and reducing ambiguity. Compared to wills, trusts are less likely to be contested, making them a reliable option for ensuring that specific wishes are followed. The explicit instructions within a trust minimize disagreements over asset distribution, helping maintain harmony and avoiding conflicts among family members. This ensures that parents' guidance continues to support their children and uphold family unity even after their lifetime.

Tax Benefits

Alongside these personal advantages, living trusts offer compelling financial incentives, especially for larger estates. While not every living trust provides tax benefits, those strategically planned can significantly reduce estate taxes. Grantors seeking to maximize their legacy can leverage these benefits, sometimes avoiding hefty tax liabilities entirely. Take, for instance, a couple with substantial holdings. By setting up a credit shelter trust—commonly part of a living trust—they can capitalize on both partners' estate tax exemptions, potentially doubling the amount passed on tax-free to their heirs. This approach not only preserves their financial legacy but also encourages strategic, informed decision-making, underscoring the importance of comprehensive, tailored financial planning.

When considering a living trust, it's vital to recognize it as part of a broader estate management strategy. Unlike other estate tools, a trust provides a level of control and foresight unique to its structure. It serves as a protective mechanism, not just a means of distributing wealth, ensuring your personal and financial interests remain safeguarded.

In sum, whether avoiding probate's complexities or equipping your heirs with well-structured financial security, living trusts present a flexible, powerful estate planning tool. They provide a versatile framework tailored to safeguard your family's future, offering peace of mind and continuity through life's unpredictable nature. As you start to understand these benefits, the next step is to learn about how to create a living trust. This will help you see how each part works together to manage your estate effectively, making sure your plans last over time.

Components and Structure of a Living Trust

The primary components of a living trust include the grantor, the trustee, and the beneficiaries, each essential to establishing the trust's framework. Understanding the structure and components of a living trust is essential for effective asset management and ensuring that one's wishes are fulfilled.

Grantor

Trusting someone's knowledge and decisions is fundamental to the structure of a living trust. The grantor establishes the terms and conditions that govern how assets will be managed and distributed. A lack of clarity in outlining these conditions can create ambiguity, potentially causing disputes or deviations from the grantor's intentions. Clear and detailed instructions, covering aspects like asset allocation and timing of distributions, ensure that the grantor's wishes are carried out accurately and their legacy remains intact.

Consider an example: A grantor sets up a living trust with a clause that allows for the distribution of certain assets only upon a beneficiary reaching a certain age. This decision reflects careful thought into the potential needs of the beneficiary, offering them security at a point when they're equipped to manage the assets responsibly. Such foresight depends on the grantor's clarity in envisioning the future course of their assets and ensuring that every decision aligns with their wishes and values.

Trustee

The trustee, chosen by the grantor, manages the trust and protects the beneficiaries' interests. This role demands integrity, diligence, and a deep commitment to the grantor's outlined wishes. Selection of a trustee can range from a family member who intimately understands the grantor's intentions to a professional entity with a proven track record in managing trusts. Regardless, the trustee's fiduciary duties can't be overstated. They must prioritize beneficiaries' well-being above all else, often making financial decisions, handling distributions, or managing the day-to-day administration of the trust.

For example, a trusted lawyer is named as a trustee, given their expertise and understanding of the grantor's family dynamics. In this situation, the lawyer might assess market conditions to decide the best time to sell an asset, ensuring the beneficiaries receive maximum value. Alternatively, consider a family member as a trustee. They possess an advantage in their understanding of individual beneficiary needs. However, their critical ability lies in their decision-making skills, which ensure that every move aligns with preserving the trust's value and honoring the grantor's intentions. Thus, choosing the right trustee can directly influence the efficacy and harmony throughout the trust's lifetime.

Beneficiaries

Beneficiaries, often at the top of the mind in estate planning, are another component in the framework of a living trust. The importance of identifying them clearly and understanding their roles and rights cannot be overstated. Clarity in naming ensures no ambiguity in understanding who benefits and to what extent. Such specificity helps avoid potential conflicts, ensuring that the grantor's intentions are unambiguously represented in the trust's instructions. When a grantor names grandchildren as contingent beneficiaries, they illustrate the trust's flexibility and intent to benefit future generations. This decision reflects the value placed on legacy, considering not just immediate family, but also the long-term well-being of descendants.

Trust Document

Throughout the living trust framework, the importance of the trust document itself cannot be overlooked. This document serves as the legal blueprint guiding every action within the trust. It outlines the assets, defines trustee roles, and provides clear distribution instructions. The precision in drafting this document ensures all parties understand and adhere to the grantor's wishes unequivocally. For example, specifying conditions under which distributions may be made, such as milestones or specific circumstances, offers a clear pathway, ensuring everyone involved anticipates and understands the decision-making process.

Using concrete language and addressing potential contingencies ensures the trust document supports comprehensive and informed planning. For instance, a trust document that includes provisions for special needs beneficiaries helps maintain their eligibility for government benefits. Incorporating specific language protects their care while avoiding any risk of disrupting available public support. In another instance, a carefully worded directive might allow for modification of the trust should tax laws change, preserving the tax benefits initially intended by the grantor. Through such foresight in drafting, the trust embodies flexibility and robustness, prepared to adapt while remaining firmly aligned with the grantor's core objectives.

Understanding these components within a living trust enables you to effectively leverage its advantages over other estate planning tools. Focusing on the grantor's pivotal role, ensuring the trustee's integrity and capability, carefully selecting beneficiaries, and precisely formulating the trust document collectively contribute to creating a balanced and effective estate plan. Each component works together to ensure clarity, reliability, and long-term success. When all parts are thoughtfully integrated and clearly articulated, they collectively uphold the grantor's legacy, serving future generations as intended.

Conclusion

As we wrap up our exploration of living trusts, it's clear that these tools offer a unique blend of control and flexibility, making them an appealing choice for many looking to safeguard their legacy. Understanding how living trusts work—offering probate avoidance, asset management during incapacity, privacy, and tailored distributions—helps you effectively manage your estate planning needs. Embracing this knowledge equips you to make thoughtful decisions about your future, maximizing the benefits for yourself and your loved ones while minimizing stress and uncertainty.

In the next chapter, we will discuss everything regarding estate planning and the common myths related to it.

Chapter 2: Estate Planning Basics

Sarah always believed that her financial affairs would take care of themselves. She had a modest savings account, a small house, and cherished keepsakes she intended to pass on to her children. But when her older sister, Mary, passed away suddenly without a clear estate plan, Sarah witnessed firsthand the chaos and heartache it brought to their family. Disputes over Mary's belongings led to strained relationships and drawn-out legal processes. This experience left an indelible impression on Sarah about the importance of having a well-prepared estate plan.

For many, estate planning seems like an overwhelming task meant only for the wealthy or elderly. However, as Sarah realized, it is a critical step for anyone who wishes to protect their assets and spare their loved ones from unnecessary stress. In this chapter, we will explore the fundamental concepts of estate planning, providing clarity on its significance and how proactive measures can lead to smoother transitions for your heirs.

Purpose of Estate Planning

Estate planning might sound formal and perhaps a bit daunting, but it's a practical step for ensuring clarity and direction when distributing assets. At its core, it's about preparing for the future and ensuring your wishes are carried out according to your desires. When everything is mapped out ahead of time, it not only brings peace of mind during your life but also spares your loved ones unnecessary stress and potential conflicts after your passing.

Understanding Responsibilities

Proactive planning starts with defining roles, especially for executors and trustees. These individuals carry the responsibility of implementing your wishes, making their understanding of their duties vital. You can avoid confusion by clearly communicating these roles. The burden on your family significantly lessens when those chosen to execute the plan know precisely what to do and how to do it.

For example, an executor tasked with managing an estate knows they're responsible for settling debts, distributing assets, and tying up any loose ends. If the instructions are clear, there's less room for misinterpretation. Take the scenario of a family that avoided long-standing disagreements simply because the roles and responsibilities of the plan were defined early and understood by all involved. It provides comfort and support for your loved ones during challenging times, ensuring they are cared for when they need it most.

Risk Management

Next, let's explore risk management within an estate plan. Life, full of unpredictability, often demands safety for the unforeseen. Estate planning helps mitigate risks such as potential incapacity. An estate plan that's thorough covers bases like healthcare proxies and durable powers of attorney, necessary for those times one might not be able to make decisions independently. Addressing these issues in your estate plan not only protects your assets but also ensures that decisions align with your intentions.

Let us consider a story that will illustrate the chaos that ensues when there's no risk management in place: siblings arguing over medical decisions during a parent's incapacity. The stress of these moments can strain relationships, but with a comprehensive estate plan, it can be as simple as referring back to agreed-upon directives. Mitigating future conflicts helps in avoiding legal battles and strengthens family bonds because everyone knows their role when challenges arise.

Providing for Loved Ones

Estate planning has a vital role in providing for loved ones, particularly the financial security of minors or dependents. When you allocate resources according to needs, you ensure their financial well-being along with preserving family legacies and traditions. Consider the influence of a well-thought-out plan for children. Monthly stipends and educational funds guarantee that what's left behind supports the future generations adequately without placing undue financial burden on others.

For instance, a grandparent's forethought in establishing a college fund for grandchildren can mean the difference between limited educational opportunities and those youngsters graduating debt-free. The flexibility in how assets get distributed allows specific allocations that directly benefit individuals, sustaining a family's legacy and traditions over time.

When everyone understands the why and how behind decisions, it's easier to maintain stability. Instead of disputes, there's gratitude and appreciation for what's been left behind.

With estate planning in place, you secure a legacy that speaks to your values, desires, and hopes for the future. As this section on estate planning wraps up, your understanding of its vital components prepares you for practical implementation. Looking ahead, the next section will discuss the use and differences between Wills and Trusts, Powers of Attorney, Healthcare Directives, and Asset Inventories.

Key Elements of a Comprehensive Estate Plan

A comprehensive estate plan involves various essential components designed to safeguard your assets, ensure clarity, and provide peace of mind for you and your loved ones. Each element serves a distinct purpose in creating a cohesive framework that reflects your intentions.

Powers of Attorney

Assigning powers of attorney is a critical step in estate planning. This legal document designates a trusted individual to make decisions on your behalf if you are incapacitated. Whether for financial or healthcare matters, powers of attorney ensure that someone you trust is empowered to act in your best interests.

Clearly defining the scope of authority granted through powers of attorney minimizes potential conflicts. When decision-making responsibilities are explicitly outlined, it reduces ambiguity and ensures that your wishes are respected. This arrangement not only protects your personal and financial interests but also provides peace of mind, knowing that your affairs are in capable hands.

Healthcare Directives

Healthcare directives, often referred to as advance directives, are vital documents that outline your medical preferences in situations where you are unable to communicate them. These directives guide healthcare professionals in providing the care you desire, ranging from treatment options to end-of-life decisions.

In emergencies, advance directives alleviate the burden on family members, helping them make difficult medical choices with confidence. They ensure that your wishes regarding medical interventions are clearly conveyed, reducing uncertainty and stress during challenging times. Healthcare directives demonstrate your proactive approach to planning for unforeseen circumstances.

Asset Inventory

Creating an inventory of assets is an important organizational step in estate planning. An asset inventory is essentially a detailed list of all your possessions, including properties, bank accounts, investments, and personal belongings. This list simplifies the identification and distribution of assets among beneficiaries.

Organized and up-to-date asset inventories provide clarity about your estate's contents and ensure that no asset is overlooked during the planning process. When beneficiaries and their respective responsibilities are clearly defined, it minimizes confusion and potential disputes. An asset inventory forms the backbone of a transparent estate plan, facilitating smooth transitions and equitable distribution.

Each component of a comprehensive estate plan contributes to maintaining control over your affairs and ensuring that decisions align with your intentions. Powers of attorney safeguard your interests when you cannot act independently. Healthcare directives make your medical preferences known and ease emotional strain on loved ones. Asset inventories bring structure and transparency to asset management and distribution.

Estate planning is not solely about managing legalities. It aims to provide support, clarity, and reassurance for you and your family during critical moments. Taking these proactive measures helps prevent conflicts and ensures that your wishes are carried out seamlessly.

A well-rounded estate plan incorporates these elements to address key aspects of decision-making, healthcare preferences, and asset management. Thoughtful planning reflects your care for your loved ones, sparing them from unnecessary stress while preserving your legacy. Understanding the significance of powers of attorney, healthcare directives, and asset inventories empowers you to create an estate plan that fulfills your goals and provides long-term peace of mind.

Importance of Regularly Updating Plans

In our journey through estate planning, we've already understood the essentials of legal documents like wills, living trusts, health care proxies, and financial powers of attorney. These tools form the backbone of any robust estate plan. But understanding these documents is only one piece of the puzzle. Estate planning is not a one-and-done deal and must evolve with the changes in your life and the world around you.

As you work with these documents, it's important to remember that life is ever-changing. Adaptability and understanding the fluid nature of circumstances can help ensure your work remains relevant and impactful. Families are dynamic. Financial circumstances shift, and laws are continually being revised. This ever-changing landscape calls for regular updates to your estate plan. Let's explore why these updates matter so much and how they can play a pivotal role in safeguarding your wishes and your loved ones' futures.

Life Changes

Let's consider alterations in personal life. Take, for instance, a couple who recently expanded their family with the birth of a child. Suddenly, their priorities shift significantly. The couple might consider appointing a guardian for their child if the unexpected happens. This addition to their family demands an update to their estate plan to address new responsibilities and emotional concerns.

Similarly, changes like marriage or divorce mean revisiting your plan. A marriage might introduce new assets or change your view on how you want your assets distributed. On the other hand, divorce often necessitates removing an ex-spouse from positions of power within your plan, such as executor or power of attorney. These personal life changes show how essential it is to maintain an estate plan that reflects current circumstances.

Legal Changes

Beyond personal life intricacies, legislation impacts estate planning. Laws don't stay static. Tax legislation changes, and so do regulations around inheritance and estate management. When laws change, they can have a direct impact on how estates are taxed or how assets are transferred. It's not hard to see how a plan that abides by old laws might unintentionally create tax liabilities or distribution issues that could have otherwise been avoided with an update.

Financial Changes

Financial circumstances are another area requiring vigilance. Consider someone who comes into a significant inheritance or experiences a windfall from a business venture. These new financial realities also demand adjustments to an estate plan. Without updates, you might overlook opportunities for tax-efficient gifting or protection from creditors.

Conversely, if someone experiences a financial downturn, their estate plan may need amendments to account for diminished assets, avoiding complications when assets listed in the will no longer exist.

Family Dynamics

Family dynamics further contribute to the complexity of estate planning. Relationships change over time, and with them, the dynamics within a family. Perhaps you have fallen out with a once-trusted friend or family member who was slated to take on the role of executor. Or maybe a new relationship blossoms, and you want to ensure this new individual is recognized in your plans. Keeping your estate plan up-to-date shows respect for evolving relationships and ensures your intentions remain aligned with your feelings.

Regular updates protect your desires but also help prevent potential disputes. Family disagreements over estates often result from ambiguous or outdated plans. Clarifying your intentions leaves little room for interpretation and can prevent misunderstandings that might otherwise lead to long, drawn-out legal battles among your loved ones. For example, detailed guidance and updated executorships can prevent disputes during difficult times.

Take Sarah, a hypothetical figure who adjusted her estate plan when her son graduated from college. Beforehand, her will left everything to her husband. But knowing that her son had now reached an age of financial maturity, Sarah amended her plan to include contributions to her son's new business ventures. Without this update, his interests and promising career startup might never have received the support intended.

Regularly updating your estate plan is as much about legacy as it is about logistical accuracy. You make sure that your values and priorities are accurately represented and carried forward by revisiting your plan. It reflects a commitment to careful consideration of how your lifelong work should continue supporting and empowering future generations, according to your current vision.

When we examine each aspect—personal life changes, legislative revisions, financial shifts, and family dynamics—the importance of maintaining an up-to-date estate plan becomes unquestionable. Each requires deliberate attention and proactive management to ensure that what you leave behind is in line with your intentions. Moreover, keeping a plan with continuous updates positions you to make informed decisions, ensuring compliance while embracing all that life brings.

In a world of constant change, think of your estate plan as a living document. It's not only about what you leave behind but also how you represent your journey and relationships at every stage. You have the power to harness these updates, upholding your legacy in a way that truly honors your life's work and intentions. Take control and adapt your estate plan to the nuances of your life; It will help avoid conflict, fit your current situation, and reflect your story even after you're gone.

Common Estate Planning Documents

Estate planning is required to ensure your wishes are respected and your loved ones are cared for during life's uncertainties or after your passing. Navigating the essential documents can simplify the process and provide lasting peace of mind. Below are key estate planning documents that form a comprehensive framework.

Last Will and Testament

A last will and testament outlines how assets will be distributed after death, making it essential for estate planning. This document provides clarity on property allocation and defines guardianship for minor children, safeguarding their future in case of unforeseen events. Including precise legal requirements, such as formal signatures and witnesses, ensures the validity of the will and reduces the risk of disputes.

This document serves as a roadmap for managing affairs, minimizing confusion for loved ones. Establishing a comprehensive will offers both security and peace of mind, while helping families avoid unnecessary legal battles and delays.

Living Trusts

Living trusts allow individuals to manage assets during their lifetime and ensure seamless distribution afterward. Unlike wills, trusts bypass the probate process, allowing direct asset transfer to beneficiaries. This approach saves time, reduces costs, and minimizes emotional strain during periods of loss.

Trusts also provide privacy, as their terms and distributions are not subject to public scrutiny, unlike wills that go through probate. This feature is particularly valuable for families concerned about maintaining discretion in financial matters. Furthermore, living trusts are beneficial for minors and individuals with special needs, allowing structured asset management until they can handle their inheritance independently.

Setting up and funding a trust requires careful planning to maximize its benefits. Assets must be transferred into the trust during the grantor's lifetime to ensure its effectiveness. Using living trusts thoughtfully creates smoother transitions and secures the privacy of financial dealings.

Health Care Proxy

A health care proxy designates a trusted individual to make medical decisions in critical situations. This document ensures that a person's medical preferences are respected when they cannot communicate their wishes themselves.

Providing specific directives in advance reduces emotional stress for family members during difficult times. Proxies can make informed decisions regarding treatments, life support, and end-of-life care, following the individual's expressed desires. Ensuring clarity in these directives avoids uncertainty and helps families navigate medical challenges with confidence.

A health care proxy is vital for preventing disagreements or delays in decision-making during emergencies. Establishing one ensures that medical care aligns with the patient's values and provides families with the reassurance they need during challenging moments

Financial Power of Attorney

The financial power of attorney allows an appointed individual to handle financial affairs in case of incapacity. Tasks such as paying bills, managing investments, and accessing resources are conducted efficiently through this arrangement, preventing potential financial crises.

Clear limitations and specific guidelines are essential to prevent misuse of authority. These boundaries define the scope within which the appointed individual can act, safeguarding the principal's assets from mismanagement. This document provides confidence that financial matters remain orderly and ensures that loved ones avoid unnecessary stress during challenging circumstances.

A financial power of attorney is particularly important for individuals with extensive investments or complex portfolios. Allowing someone to act swiftly during incapacitation ensures continuity and stability in financial management.

Each document contributes uniquely to estate planning, establishing an effective and secure framework. The last will and testament ensures clear asset distribution and guardianship provisions. Living trusts simplify transitions, protect privacy, and provide structured management for beneficiaries. Health care proxies alleviate emotional burdens by ensuring medical decisions align with preferences. Financial powers of attorney safeguard resources by empowering trusted individuals to handle finances during incapacity.

Together, these tools create a thoughtful and comprehensive approach to estate planning. Individuals can craft their plans with confidence, ensuring their legacy is honored and their loved ones are supported. Familiarity with these documents lays the foundation for a secure future.

Conclusion

Now that we've explored the fundamental concepts of estate planning, you can confidently take action toward securing your legacy. Addressing risks by including healthcare proxies and powers of attorney ensures decisions are made true to your intentions, protecting both your assets and family bonds. As we move forward into examining specific tools like wills and trusts, remember that each step you take strengthens your family's future and upholds the values most important to you.

In the next chapter, we will discuss the process of creating a living trust and explore the essential aspects of trustee selection.

Interactive Myths Quiz: Challenge Your Estate Planning Knowledge

Question 1: *True or False: Estate planning is only for the wealthy.*

- **Answer:** False.
- **Explanation:** Estate planning is essential for everyone, regardless of financial status. It addresses guardianship, healthcare decisions, and allocation of modest assets.

Question 2: *What is the key difference between a will and a living trust?*

- **Answer:** A will specifies asset distribution after death, while a living trust allows asset management during life and after.
- **Explanation:** Living trusts bypass probate, offering more privacy and efficiency compared to wills.

Question 3: *True or False: Estate planning is unnecessary until you have dependents.*

- **Answer:** False.
- **Explanation:** Estate planning is vital for all adults to address healthcare decisions, incapacity, and asset management, even if they don't have dependents.

Question 4: *Which document specifies your medical treatment preferences if you're unable to communicate them?*

- **Answer:** Healthcare directive (or advance directive).
- **Explanation:** Healthcare directives guide medical professionals and family in carrying out your wishes during emergencies.

Question 5: *True or False: A durable power of attorney becomes invalid if you are incapacitated.*

- **Answer:** False.
- **Explanation:** A durable power of attorney is specifically designed to remain effective during incapacity, allowing a trusted person to make decisions on your behalf.

Question 6: *Why is an asset inventory critical in estate planning?*

- **Answer:** It provides a comprehensive list of all possessions for proper identification and distribution.
- **Explanation:** Organized inventories minimize oversight and disputes, ensuring clarity among beneficiaries.

Question 7: *True or False: Once you create an estate plan, you don't need to revisit it.*

- **Answer:** False.
- **Explanation:** Estate plans must be updated to reflect changes in personal life, finances, family dynamics, and legislation.

Question 8: *What is probate, and why might people want to avoid it?*

- **Answer:** Probate is a legal process for validating a will and distributing assets.
- **Explanation:** It can be time-consuming, costly, and public, which is why tools like living trusts are often used to bypass it.

Question 9: *True or False: Online estate planning tools are unreliable and ineffective.*

- **Answer:** False.
- **Explanation:** Many online tools offer accessible and affordable ways to create estate plans, especially for straightforward cases.

Question 10: *What common financial change could require updating your estate plan?*

Chapter 3: Creating a Living Trust: Step-by-Step

Have you ever thought about how important it is to ensure your assets are distributed according to your wishes? Many people find themselves wondering how they can protect their hard-earned wealth and provide for loved ones without involving extensive legal assistance or excessive costs. Estate planning often feels overwhelming, especially when faced with the multitude of options available. One of these options is creating a living trust—a task that might seem intimidating at first but promises peace of mind and financial security.

In this chapter, we will understand the complex yet rewarding process of setting up a living trust. You'll gain a clear understanding of selecting the right trustee, whether a trusted family member or a professional fiduciary, and learn how to navigate the responsibilities that come with it. We'll cover the steps, criteria for selection, and the implications of different choices, equipping you with the knowledge to confidently approach this vital aspect of estate planning independently.

Selecting a Trustee

The role of a trustee in managing a living trust cannot be overstated. A trustee is responsible for ensuring the trust operates according to your wishes, managing assets, paying expenses, and ultimately distributing assets to the beneficiaries. This demands financial acumen and a deep commitment to honoring the terms set out in the trust. A trustee must possess both the expertise to handle complex financial matters and the integrity to act in the trust's best interests. That makes selecting a suitable individual or organization crucial for successfully executing estate plans.

Types of Trustees

Various trustee options are available, each with distinct advantages and challenges. A family member or close friend might seem a natural choice given their understanding of personal dynamics and intentions. However, this decision carries potential emotional weight. Family members may face conflicts of interest, especially where significant assets are involved, resulting in strained relationships. Alternatively, choosing a professional fiduciary, like a bank or a trust company, offers impartiality and expertise, ensuring that the trust is managed objectively. The downside can include ongoing fees that might impact the trust's value over time. Consider a situation where a family member, well-meaning but untrained, struggles with tax complexities, jeopardizing asset preservation. Contrast this with a professional's systematic approach, where their knowledge reduces liabilities. Balancing these considerations helps in determining the best trustee option.

Criteria for Selection

When deciding on a trustee, several criteria come to the forefront.

1. **Financial experience**: The trustee must have a solid understanding of financial matters. Without this expertise, even seemingly simple financial decisions can escalate into major issues.

2. **Availability**: The trustee should have sufficient time and energy to dedicate to their responsibilities. Complex estates may demand considerable effort, so availability is essential.

3. **Willingness to serve**: It is important to select someone who is willing to take on the role. A reluctant trustee may not approach the responsibilities with the necessary diligence or commitment.

4. **Emotional intelligence**: The ability to navigate sensitive family situations with empathy and tact is crucial, especially in contexts where family harmony is a priority.

5. **Strong communication skills**: Effective communication helps prevent misunderstandings and ensures all parties involved understand the decisions and actions being taken.

6. **Mediation and conflict resolution skills**: Trustees should have the capability to mediate discussions about asset distribution, helping to avoid resentment and fostering harmony among beneficiaries.

Evaluating these criteria ensures the trustee you choose is fully prepared to manage your estate in alignment with your vision and intentions.□

Discussing Roles

Open conversations with potential trustees are essential for transparency and preventing misunderstandings. When trustees are unclear about their duties, they may act inconsistently, leading to disputes. However, clearly outlining responsibilities and addressing questions can ensure the trust operates smoothly, achieves its goals, and safeguards relationships.

Candid discussions provide clarity that reassures both the trust creator and trustee. These dialogues also allow for adjusting roles based on the individual's comfort and capability, fostering collaboration and a reliable partnership. Proactive communication ensures a shared understanding, preparing trustees both legally and emotionally to fulfill their responsibilities while uniting everyone behind the trust's purpose.

The next step is to draft the trust document, which legally records decisions like naming involved parties, listing assets, and using clear terms. This shifts from choosing the trustee to legally enabling them to fulfill your wishes. A well-crafted document ensures accuracy, includes necessary legal elements, and safeguards your estate's future.

Drafting the Trust Document

Selecting the right trustee is an important decision when setting up a living trust. Once you've made this choice, it's time to focus on drafting the trust document itself. This is where you'll put pen to paper, formalizing the roles and responsibilities already outlined. Let's understand how you can tackle this, balancing legal requirements with your understanding.

Basic Components of the Document

The main parts of any trust document are the title, purpose declaration, and identification of key people: the grantor, trustee, and beneficiaries.

- **Title**: The title is straightforward but significant, serving as the document's name. It should clearly convey the document's purpose. Think of it as the headline for your trust, announcing what's to follow.

- **Purpose declaration**: The purpose declaration articulates the trust's objectives. It should express why you're setting up the trust and what you hope to achieve. Whether it's ensuring your pets are cared for after you're gone or providing for your grandchildren's education, the purpose must be crystal clear. This clarity helps everyone involved stay focused on the trust's intentions.

- **Designation of grantor, trustee, and beneficiaries**: Naming the grantor, trustee, and beneficiaries is a critical step. Each party's identity and roles must be specifically designated within the document. Avoid ambiguity by using full, legal names and detailed descriptions of roles, as vague language can lead to complications and misunderstandings down the line. □

Legal Language Considerations

When drafting the trust, negotiating legal language is where many stumble. Legal terminology can be intimidating, so your challenge is to use it to meet legal standards without overwhelming yourself or others. Start by understanding that legal language exists to protect all parties involved, not just to confuse you. It's there for precision. Use simplified wording where possible and consider footnotes for complex terms. These footnotes can act as a valuable glossary for anyone reading who's not familiar with legal jargon. For example, if you use the term "fiduciary," a footnote can provide a quick explanation: "A fiduciary is a person who manages assets for someone else's benefit."

Templates and Resources

Templates can be very helpful in drafting the trust documents. Reputable legal websites and community resources offer templates that can guide you in structuring the document effectively. Templates offer a starting point and reduce errors by walking you through the standard format.

Aside from templates, consider tapping into community workshops. Many nonprofits and local organizations offer free or low-cost estate planning workshops. These offer helpful advice from experts and others who are in the same situation. Not only do you get a better grasp of the process, but you also connect with resources that can support you along the way.

This book includes a bonus booklet containing all the templates required for setting up a trust. These templates provide a structured starting point and help reduce errors in drafting trust documents.

Consulting Professionals

Despite your efforts to draft the document yourself, there might come a time when bringing in a professional proves beneficial. Different states have varying laws regarding trusts, and complex situations may require expert advice. Consulting a professional ensures you comply with all legal standards and avoid potential challenges. But seeking professional help doesn't mean you're negating your own efforts. It's a way to bolster your work, providing peace of mind that everything is legally sound. Even a one-time consultation can be a cost-effective strategy for polishing and finalizing your document.

When calculating costs, balancing self-drafting with professional assistance can save you significantly. Consider opting for a lawyer's review rather than paying them to draft the entire document. This approach gives you the best of both worlds: your personal touch remains intact, and you gain valuable insights from someone well-versed in the legal landscape.

Now that your trust is drafted, the next step is transferring assets into the living trust. Without this step, your trust is essentially an empty shell. Funding the trust with assets ensures it functions correctly and fulfills its purpose. Begin thinking about which assets you'll need to transfer, considering how this process protects them and secures their distribution according to your wishes.

In summary, drafting a trust document involves carefully balancing legal jargon with straightforward language. Using templates, seeking local resources, and knowing when to consult professionals allows you to create a legally sound document while retaining control over the process. Recognize the importance of each element in your trust document, ensuring you meet both legal and personal goals.

Funding the Trust

Funding the trust is an essential step because transferring assets into it ensures the trust can serve its intended purpose effectively. The purpose of a trust is to protect and manage your assets, but this cannot happen unless the trust is funded adequately. A secure vault can only fulfill its purpose when treasures are moved inside. Without them, it remains an empty and decorative structure, unable to serve its intended function. Similarly, funding a trust involves moving your assets into it, thereby breathing life into its provisions and enabling trustees to carry out your wishes effectively.

Process of Funding

Let's break down the process of transferring assets to understand what this step entails. Different assets require different methods for transferring titles to the trust, and understanding these variations is key. For real estate, the process typically involves retitling the deed in the name of the trust. Legal documents will list your trust as the new proprietor, making the transition official. Similarly, when moving bank accounts or investments, you'll need to complete forms—sometimes provided by the institution—to list the trust as the account holder. It's vital to communicate with your bank to understand its requirements for funding, as these sometimes necessitate face-to-face discussions or notarized documents.

Now, consider owning a vehicle that you wish the trust to manage. This involves changing the vehicle title to reflect the trust as the new owner, which can generally be done at the Department of Motor Vehicles. With all titled assets, the approach remains consistent yet personalized to the asset type. Consider these steps as your roadmap to confident asset transfer, paving the way for seamless trust functionality.

Transferring financial accounts into a trust can sometimes pose challenges, particularly in dealing with financial institutions unfamiliar with your specific trust arrangement. In these scenarios, proactive communication becomes your ally. By approaching these institutions with relevant documentation and a clear understanding of your trust's needs, you can collaborate to facilitate a smooth transition. For example, if a bank employee seems hesitant about naming the trust as an account holder, providing explanations and necessary paperwork can iron out the confusion. The aim is to foster a cooperative spirit that prioritizes effective and efficient asset transition, assuring that your assets align with your estate planning goals.

Documentation Requirements

Documentation and record-keeping throughout the funding process can't be overstated. This meticulousness prevents legal hiccups and ensures that the transition process adheres to your broad objectives. Essential documents like deeds, titles, beneficiary designations, or trust certifications become the lifeblood of your trust's operations when organized efficiently. It's wise to establish a comprehensive filing system that categorizes these documents clearly and maintains chronological accuracy. Label your folders and electronic files for seamless retrieval, promoting a sustainable organization model. This practice enhances accuracy and accountability, empowering you to manage and prove your transfers confidently.

Expert Guidance

Given that asset transfers can involve varied tax implications, consulting with a tax professional becomes an insightful precaution. Changes in ownership can sometimes trigger tax consequences by impacting capital gains taxation or property tax reassessment. Adopting a proactive approach by seeking expert advice helps you avoid unintended financial surprises while navigating the complex terrain of tax legislation. This consultation can offer clarity, shedding light on any adjustments needed to safeguard your fiscal interests during the funding endeavor.

Our exploration of how to transfer assets into a trust doesn't end here. Many more elements contribute to making the trust function optimally, like ample review and meticulous finalization. Verifying informational accuracy and asset listings emerges as paramount post-transfer to guarantee your trust accurately mirrors your estate plans. Next, we'll understand the nuances of this finalization process. Ensuring that all involved parties sign the correct documents and comply with state laws becomes the topic of our subsequent discussion. So while funding gives the trust its momentum, refining its operation and integration into your broader estate plans beckons as your next logical step. Let's prepare to make every detail count .

Review and Finalization

Creating a living trust is a vital step in securing your assets and ensuring your wishes are honored, but the final steps are equally important to ensure it's complete and legally sound. Here's how to navigate this critical phase:

Final Review Points

Before considering your trust complete, it's essential to double-check every detail. Verify the accuracy of all information and asset listings. Mistakes here can lead to complications down the road. Ensure all required signatures are obtained, solidifying the trust's legality. Additionally, review compliance with state laws to avoid any future legal issues. Taking the time to thoroughly inspect these elements ensures your trust is valid and effective.

Communicating with Family

Once your trust is finalized, discussing it with family members and beneficiaries is key. Sharing the details of the trust fosters transparency and reassures loved ones about future distributions. Encourage open conversations and allow beneficiaries to ask questions, so they fully understand their roles and responsibilities. Open communication can help minimize potential misunderstandings or conflicts in the event of incapacity or death, creating a smoother path forward for everyone involved.

Storing the Trust Document

Safe storage of your trust document is essential for its durability and accessibility. Consider whether digital storage or physical copies suit your needs best—both options have advantages. Ensure trusted individuals, such as family members or financial advisors, know how to access the document if needed. Sharing copies with key stakeholders can further protect its security and ensure everyone involved is prepared.

Conclusion

Having explored the essential steps for setting up a living trust independently, it becomes clear that selecting the right trustee plays a pivotal role in ensuring your estate is managed according to your intentions. With a deep understanding of the criteria for choosing a trustee and the benefits and challenges of different options, you are now well-equipped to move forward confidently. The steps you've taken so far will lead you into the practical execution of these plans, turning thoughtful preparation into actionable estate management.

In the next chapter, we will uncover how living trusts serve as an effective alternative to the challenges of probate. The focus will be on simplifying estate transfers, reducing legal complexities, and easing emotional burdens for families.

Worksheet: Selecting the Right Trustee

Here's a guide to help you in evaluating and selecting the most suitable trustee for your living trust.

Step 1: Identify Potential Trustees

List potential candidates (individuals or organizations) for consideration:
Examples: Family member, close friend, professional fiduciary, bank, or trust company.

1. ______________________________
2. ______________________________
3. ______________________________
4. ______________________________
5. ______________________________
6. ______________________________
7. ______________________________
8. ______________________________
9. ______________________________
10. ______________________________

Step 2: Trustee Evaluation Table

Evaluate each candidate based on essential criteria. Use a scale from 1 (poor) to 5 (excellent) to rate their suitability.

Criteria	Candidate Name 1	Candidate Name 2	Candidate Name 3
Financial Experience			
Availability			
Willingness to Serve			
Emotional Intelligence			
Communication Skills			
Mediation Skills			
Overall Rating	(Sum of Scores)	(Sum of Scores)	(Sum of Scores)

Tip: Focus on candidates who score consistently high across multiple criteria.

Step 3: Scenario Reflection

Imagine how each candidate might handle specific situations. Write down your thoughts.

- **Scenario 1**: Managing disagreements among beneficiaries.□
  How would each candidate approach this situation?

____

- **Scenario 2**: Handling complex financial decisions, such as tax planning or property distribution.□
  Who has the expertise and demeanor to navigate such challenges?

____

- **Scenario 3**: Balancing fairness while honoring your wishes.□

Who is the most impartial and trustworthy?

____

Step 4: Communication

Answer the following prompts to finalize your decision:

1. Have you discussed the responsibilities of the trustee role with each candidate?

____

2. Are they comfortable and willing to take on this responsibility?

____

3. Do they understand your expectations and goals for the trust?

____

Step 5: Decision

Based on your evaluation and conversations, write down your selected trustee(s):

Name of Trustee(s): ________________________

Chapter 4: Avoiding Probate

Losing a loved one brings both emotional and practical challenges, often requiring you to navigate complex legal processes during a time of grief. Take the example of Sarah, who found herself amid probate proceedings after her father's passing. Along with handling her sorrow, she had to sift through paperwork filled with unfamiliar terms about debts and asset distribution. Court dates and administrative fees began to consume her time and diminish the inheritance. On top of this, disagreements among family members over who should receive what caused additional strain, further complicating an already difficult situation.

For families like Sarah's, these experiences highlight the often unpredictable and stressful nature of dealing with probate without prior planning. Unfortunately, many people think they have no choice but to face probate's logistical and emotional challenges. However, understanding alternatives could change this perspective. In this chapter, we'll explore how living trusts can help avoid such ordeals, offering smoother paths for estate transfers as we discuss the practical strategies to sidestep the complexities of probate.

Understanding Probate and Its Implications

Probate can be daunting for many, especially when navigating the aftermath of a loved one's passing. Essentially, probate is a legal procedure for distributing a deceased person's estate, ensuring all debts and taxes are settled, and the remaining assets are appropriately distributed according to the will or state law. On paper, this sounds straightforward, yet it often entails a drawn-out affair involving legal paperwork, court supervision, and sometimes an emotional toll on families who are already grieving.

Consequences of Probate

One of the main criticisms of the probate process is its sheer duration. Even simple estates can take months to pass through probate, while more complex cases might stretch over several years. Factors like backlog in courts, handling offbeat assets, or disagreements among heirs only add to the time. When you factor in the need for court appearances, the pressure mounts. Families are often left in limbo during this period, unable to access inheritance or emotional closure.

The financial burden of probate also raises eyebrows. Courts usually demand a portion of the estate's value as fees, besides additional costs such as attorney fees. In some situations, these could add up to 3% to 7% of the entire estate price tag, not to mention extra fees for appraisers or account practitioners. Moreover, these payments are typically remitted before heirs receive anything, effectively diminishing the estate and stripping families of their rightful inheritance. For estates with mounting debts, it complicates matters further since these fees dwindle the pot before distributing what's left.

The probate process often delays asset distribution, leading to uncertainty and disputes among beneficiaries over sentimental and tangible assets. These delays can strain family relationships, sometimes causing lasting rifts, despite probate's intent to protect the estate's systematic disbursement.

Common Misunderstandings

Many people aren't aware that with careful planning, probate isn't an obligatory path. It's mistakenly construed that all estates must weather probate, but the truth is, proactive estate management can avert probate altogether. Living trusts offer a viable alternative since assets placed into such trusts aren't deemed part of the estate at death, thus sidestepping probate. A trustee takes over control of your assets upon your demise, bypassing the legal rigmarole entirely.

Incorporating property ownership strategies also presents another probate-avoidance tactic. Establishing joint ownership, particularly "right of survivorship," ensures that when an owner passes, the property instantaneously transfers to any surviving co-owner, leaving no room for probate intrusion. Also, if appropriately structured, beneficiary designations on accounts like insurance or retirement funds can steer clear of probate because they automatically transfer ownership to listed beneficiaries.

Unveiling common misconceptions, it's vital to dismiss the belief that estate planning is for healthier, wealthier folk. Everyone, regardless of asset value, can benefit from planning. Trust arrangements can be scaled to modest or extensive estates alike. It's this flexibility that lays the foundation for circumventing probate, which is often overlooked as people fail to grasp how public and unfavorable probate proceedings can become without a plan.

Transferring assets during one's lifetime is another option. This practice not only warms hearts and strengthens bonds but also effectively diminishes the taxable estate size. Assigning heirs' chosen assets now negates future probate processes. Nevertheless, this avenue requires caution since there's the federal gift tax to consider, and any premature gifts could influence personal finances.

As probate can seem impersonal and disheartening, it also has cultural implications. Legal costs can deplete your wealth, and family heirlooms can become tied up in disputes. Whether tangible treasures or timeless traditions, the probate aftermath can interfere with what families consider their lasting legacy. Stepping into an anticipatory frame of mind through thoughtful planning brings peace of mind.

This mindset shift towards proactive planning can ensure family histories and legacies pass on smoothly to future generations. Exploring probate intricacies and available options helps protect cherished memories and family harmony.

As we edge towards practical steps for probate avoidance, understand the value of setting up living trusts. Establishing trusts ensures your wishes and life's work are protected in a legally binding way, avoiding courtroom delays. Exploring property strategies like lifetime gifting and proper titling strengthens probate prevention. Gradual modifications in asset management offer potential to mitigate unforeseen turbulence tomorrow, promoting a smoother transition today.

Strategies to Avoid Probate

Probate can be a daunting process, with its complications and potential for lengthy delays. But by understanding and implementing a few strategic estate planning measures, you can significantly reduce or even eliminate the need for your loved ones to go through probate when the inevitable happens. Let's understand some actionable steps you can take to avoid this cumbersome legal process, ensuring a smoother transition of your estate.

Establishing a Living Trust

One of the foundational strategies for bypassing probate is establishing a living trust. When you create a living trust, you effectively set up a legal entity to hold ownership of your assets. This means that you, as the creator or trustor, no longer own these assets in your personal capacity. Instead, the trust owns them, and you manage the trust as the trustee. Upon your death, the successor trustee you appointed takes over management and can transfer the assets directly to your beneficiaries without court interference. This eliminates the need for probate, allowing your beneficiaries to access the assets quickly. Living trusts offer flexibility and control, letting you make changes as circumstances evolve, solidifying their place as a powerful tool in modern estate planning.

Effective Property Ownership Strategies

Another hands-on strategy involves property ownership structures. Consider the option of joint ownership with the right of survivorship. When property is jointly owned, it automatically passes to the surviving owner(s) upon one owner's death, without the need for probate. This ownership form is common in real estate and banking accounts and offers a seamless transfer process. With this setup, you essentially empower the next owner to take control without dealing with the probate process, offering clarity and peace of mind through a simplified estate transition.

Utilizing Beneficiary Designations

Financial accounts and life insurance policies represent another area where you can employ beneficiary designations to sidestep probate. Assigning specific beneficiaries to your accounts ensures the funds are directed to the intended recipients upon your passing. These designations allow for a direct transfer of the assets to your heirs, effectively mitigating the legal entanglement that probate often brings. This straightforward approach provides clarity, allowing your intended wishes to be executed with minimal legal interference, highlighting the simplicity and practicality of this probate-avoidance strategy.

Gifting During Lifetime

You might also consider gifting assets during your lifetime. By doing so, you can reduce the size of your estate now, diminishing the portion subject to probate later. When engaging in gifting, it's essential to be aware of legal limits, such as the annual exclusion for gift taxes, to maximize the tax advantages without running afoul of tax regulations. Beyond the practical financial benefits, gifting assets can provide emotional rewards by allowing you to witness the positive impact of your generosity on family and loved ones. It also fosters communication about your intentions, potentially reducing family disputes after your passing.

Incorporating these approaches empowers you and your beneficiaries, helping to manage your estate proactively, efficiently, and honorably. Engage these strategies thoughtfully in your estate planning efforts today, ensuring that your intentions are clear and the transitions seamless for those you leave behind.

As we move to the next section focusing on living trusts, recognize their particular strength in avoiding probate. Living trusts function dynamically, accommodating various life circumstances, including incapacitation. Trusts manage your affairs privately, keeping your financial dealings out of public probate records, offering a level of discretion and confidentiality that probate cannot. This privacy, combined with the trust's ability to transfer assets swiftly and securely, highlights their importance in effective estate planning.

Role of Living Trusts in Probate Avoidance

Let's understand how Living Trusts work, why they're beneficial, and why many folks consider them an important of avoiding probate.

When you create a living trust, you transfer ownership of your assets to the trust. You're often the trustee while you're alive. When you pass, a successor trustee takes over, letting them distribute your assets rapidly and efficiently, without the delay of probate. This kind of swift transition to beneficiaries is priceless. It ensures that those you care for get what they're entitled to straightaway, without the wait and hassle.

Management During Incapacity

One of the often-overlooked perks of a living trust is how it accounts for managing your assets if you're incapacitated. Say you end up in a situation where you can't make decisions for yourself. Your living trust has you covered, providing clear guidelines on handling your assets without needing courts to step in. This foresight in estate planning brings peace of mind, knowing that your affairs won't fall into chaos should you become unable to manage them.

Think of a scenario where Ryan, a 65-year-old retiree, sets up a living trust to secure his assets, including his house, investments, and savings. Years later, Ryan suffers a stroke and becomes unable to manage his financial affairs. However, thanks to his living trust, Ryan has already designated his daughter, Paige, as the successor trustee. This allows Paige to step in seamlessly and manage Ryan's assets according to the instructions laid out in the trust.

With the living trust in place, Paige can ensure Ryan's medical bills are paid promptly, his investments are monitored, and his household expenses are covered, all without the intervention of a court. The clear management instructions in Ryan's trust prevent delays or legal disputes, providing his family with stability during a challenging time.

Privacy Considerations

Privacy is another aspect of living trusts. Probate proceedings are public, so anyone can look into your estate details. But trusts are private. This privacy can be very important for many people, especially if you're trying to protect private family matters or want to keep your financial information away from others.

Consider Roger, a successful entrepreneur who has built a thriving business over the years. He wants to ensure that his assets, including his business shares and personal savings, are passed on to his children without drawing unnecessary attention to his estate. If Roger relies solely on a will, his estate would go through probate, making details about his assets, beneficiaries, and business public knowledge. This could attract unwanted scrutiny, potential disputes, or even attempts to challenge his wishes.

However, by creating a living trust, Roger secures his privacy. The trust allows his children to inherit his business shares and savings discreetly, with no public records of the asset distribution. This confidentiality not only shields his family from public scrutiny but also ensures the smooth transfer of his legacy. Roger's decision to use a living trust highlights the importance of privacy in estate planning for individuals who value discretion and wish to protect their family from unnecessary complications.

Continuous Control and Flexibility

Furthermore, living trusts are flexible. Life changes, and so can your trust. Want to add a beneficiary, or even revoke the whole trust? No problem. This adaptability encourages you to stay engaged in your estate planning. You don't feel trapped by the decisions you've made; you sense the freedom to alter your plans as your life evolves.

Consider a scenario where someone has created a living trust and later decides to sell a piece of property within it. They can do so without fuss, maybe to help out a family member or invest in something new. This kind of freedom in making choices without extra obstacles shows how much control you have with a living trust.

Living trusts help you avoid probate while adding clarity and peace to your estate plan. They adapt to life's changes, protect your family's future with privacy and efficiency, and let you stay in control of your assets. Whether you're new to estate planning or updating your plans, living trusts are a practical and thoughtful choice.

Conclusion

Avoiding probate simplifies the transfer of assets, reduces family stress, and preserves privacy, ensuring a smoother journey for loved ones. Strategies like living trusts, joint ownership, beneficiary designations, and lifetime gifting are powerful tools that offer clarity and efficiency during difficult times. Remember, probate is not inevitable. Thoughtful planning empowers you to sidestep its challenges, protecting your family's future and ensuring your legacy reflects care and foresight. Take the time now to craft an estate plan that prioritizes ease, privacy, and compassion for those who matter most.

In the next chapter, we will explore strategies for managing assets within a living trust. From creating a comprehensive asset inventory to ensuring cherished family heirlooms are protected, we'll guide you in establishing a clear and secure financial future for your family.

Checklist: Key Steps to Avoiding Probate

This checklist will guide you through actionable steps to apply probate avoidance strategies effectively:

Step 1: Assess Your Assets

- ☐ Have you created a complete list of your assets (e.g., real estate, accounts, investments)?
- ☐ Have you determined the ownership status of each asset?

Step 2: Explore Living Trust Options

- ☐ Have you consulted with an estate planning professional to set up a living trust?
- ☐ Have you assigned a reliable successor trustee for your living trust?

Step 3: Use Beneficiary Designations

- ☐ Are your life insurance policies and retirement accounts updated with beneficiaries?
- ☐ Have you verified the accuracy of your beneficiary designations?

Step 4: Simplify Property Transfers

- ☐ Have you considered joint ownership with the right of survivorship for key properties?
- ☐ Have you checked your state's laws regarding property titling options?

Step 5: Plan for Incapacity

- □ Have you included provisions in your living trust to manage assets if you become incapacitated?
- □ Have you informed your family and trustees about your plans?

Step 6: Keep Your Plan Updated

- □ Are you reviewing and updating your estate plan every 2–3 years or after major life changes?
- □ Have you communicated changes clearly to your beneficiaries and trustee?

Chapter 5: Managing Assets within a Living Trust

Stacks of paperwork can feel daunting, especially when you're trying to ensure your family's future wellbeing. It's common to struggle with understanding your assets and how they fit into the bigger picture of estate planning. Questions often arise—have all your assets been accounted for, and are those cherished family heirlooms truly protected? Concerns about your children handling future responsibilities or potential disputes over asset distribution might linger in your mind.

In this chapter, we'll discuss about managing your assets within a living trust. We'll break down effective strategies to help you create a detailed asset inventory that ensures clarity and reduces confusion for your heirs. By the end, you'll have a clearer picture of how each asset contributes to a secure financial future for your family.

Asset Inventory Creation

Knowing how to compile a detailed asset inventory is essential for managing assets effectively within a living trust. A comprehensive inventory ensures clarity, minimizes disputes, and helps in smooth transitions within the trust. You lay a strong foundation for informed decision-making by understanding what assets are owned, their current status, and how they align with your estate goals. This detailed preparation not only simplifies the management process but also ensures that your trust functions as intended, offering peace of mind and efficiency.

Identifying Your Assets

To start, identifying and listing all assets is the first essential step. You'll need to consider tangible assets like your family home, any other real estate, cars, or valuable jewelry. Don't overlook personal possessions that, while seemingly minor, hold financial or emotional value. Alongside these, financial assets such as bank accounts, stocks, bonds, and retirement accounts must be included. Recognizing what constitutes an asset might extend to digital assets like your online businesses, bitcoin, or social media profiles that could generate income. All these form a part of the financial ecosystem that you're planning to protect.

Understanding the importance of knowing what counts as an asset informs better planning. When you recognize the diversity in the types of assets, you open avenues for their more effective management. For instance, appreciating how a classic car or rare coin collection fits into your estate helps in strategizing for future generations. This comprehensive awareness ensures there's clarity and helps in avoiding potential disputes among beneficiaries, as everything of value is accounted for upfront.

Valuing Your Assets

Valuing assets comes next, and not many realize how critical this step is. Accurate valuation reflects the true worth of the assets when they are eventually included in the trust. For instance, if the estimated worth of real estate differs from its market value, it can distort the overall perception of the estate's value. For beneficiaries, this precise information shapes their understanding of their financial position.

When values are accurate, communication with potential beneficiaries becomes easier and more transparent. It prevents misconceptions and, importantly, allows informed decision-making, such as whether a beneficiary might wish to hold, sell, or invest in the asset. Attaching a value to the family estate, stock portfolio, or jewelry collection ensures each asset's role is clearly understood within the estate plan.

Documenting Ownership

Documenting ownership of the assets is your safeguard against future legal headaches. Psychologically, having a neat pile of paperwork shows legitimacy, which beneficiaries and financial institutions alike respect. Imagine lacking proof of ownership and facing challenges that lead to legal entanglements. You can prevent such complications by organizing deeds, titles, stock certificates, or digital records, that could burden your executor or beneficiaries.

A well-documented ownership trail additionally streamlines the process of transferring assets into the trust. Without clear records, not only does it complicate transfer into a trust, but it can also delay access to assets when needed the most. In cases where assets are contested, documentation stands as a shield, preventing disputes and ensuring a smooth asset transition.

Organizing Your Inventory

Now, let's talk about organization. A system that works makes information easily accessible and understandable at a glance. You might consider digital solutions or physical filing systems, whatever keeps you on top of your estate's elements. A systematized approach encourages proactive decision-making.

Efficient organization of asset information supports ongoing revisions as your assets evolve. Life doesn't stop changing. Similarly, neither should your asset inventory. When you buy a new property or sell a business interest, a consistent habit of updating your records ensures that nothing slips between the cracks. Ultimately, it transforms the estate planning process into less of a daunting task and more of a manageable, integral part of your financial routine.

To make these concepts more tangible, let's look at a real-world scenario. Consider David, owning multiple properties, antique collections, and a thriving online business. His journey of organizing assets started with the daunting task of listing them all. By hiring an evaluator, David ensured accurate valuation. He realized that market dynamics had significantly boosted his property's worth. Later, he faced a hiccup when he found his antique ownership documentation was lacking. Correcting this saved future troubles for his heirs by fortifying his trust transfer.

Eliminating redundancy leads to clear and effective communication, ensuring each word is meaningful. Removing participle phrases helps streamline the message. Using straightforward language reduces the risk of misinterpretation, which is particularly critical in estate planning to prevent complications and lengthy disputes.

In the upcoming section, you'll explore types of assets best suited for inclusion in a trust. Real estate tops the list, given its value appreciation potential and relative stability. Financial accounts offer liquidity, while personal property—jewels, artwork—provides charm. Business interests can also integrate seamlessly, aiding in continuity planning. We will also understand how integrating various asset types within a living trust maximizes their value, setting the stage for understanding how to select and manage these diverse assets effectively.

Types of Assets Suitable for Trust Inclusion

Incorporating a variety of assets into your trust ensures seamless transfer to beneficiaries while reducing legal challenges and probate costs. Below are actionable insights into types of assets suitable for trust inclusion and practical steps to transfer them effectively.

Real Estate

Real estate is one of the most critical assets to place into a living trust. Failing to include property can lead to probate complications, resulting in delays, additional costs, and potential disputes among heirs. You ensure the following benefits by transferring real estate ownership to the trust:

- **Probate avoidance**: Property in a trust bypasses probate, saving heirs time and money.
- **Seamless ownership transition**: Upon the trustor's passing, the property moves directly to beneficiaries without administrative hurdles.
- **Legal clarity**: A deed transfer, using either a quitclaim deed or a warranty

deed, officially documents the property's transition to the trust, establishing ownership transparently.

Steps:

1. Compile property records, including deeds and mortgage details.
2. Work with a legal professional to execute a deed transfer, shifting ownership from your name to the trust's name.
3. Retain copies of all documentation for future reference and clarity.

Financial Accounts

Financial assets, such as bank accounts, investment portfolios, and retirement accounts, can be transferred to a living trust to guarantee uninterrupted access for beneficiaries. Probate processes often complicate access to these funds, but incorporating them into the trust simplifies allocation and ensures alignment with the trustor's intentions.

Benefits:

- **Uninterrupted fund access**: Beneficiaries can use the funds without waiting for probate clearance.
- **Legal protection**: Trust ownership reduces potential legal disputes over asset distribution.
- **Controlled allocation**: Funds can be managed and distributed according to specific wishes outlined in the trust.

Steps:

1. Consult your financial institution to gather the required forms for transferring accounts.
2. Update account designations, changing ownership to the trust.
3. Ensure the trust contains clear instructions for fund distribution.

Personal Property

Personal belongings, including items of sentimental value such as art, antiques, and collectibles, hold unique importance in estate planning. Including these assets in the trust prevents family disputes and ensures they are distributed according to the trustor's wishes.

Benefits:

- **Conflict avoidance**: Clear planning eliminates ambiguity, reducing family tensions.
- **Emotional consideration**: Special items receive the attention they deserve during asset allocation.
- **Detailed distribution**: Trust provisions can outline exact plans for items with significant emotional or monetary value.

Steps:

1. Inventory personal items, categorizing them by importance and value.
2. Specify in the trust how each item should be distributed.
3. Keep documentation, including appraisals for valuable items like collectibles or antiques.

Business Interests

For those who own businesses, incorporating ownership stakes into a living trust is essential to protect business assets and facilitate smooth transition management. Business interests often require careful planning to ensure continuity and minimize disputes among heirs.

Benefits:

- **Asset protection**: Business holdings stay secure from legal challenges.
- **Smooth transition**: Trust arrangements outline succession plans, ensuring operational continuity.

- **Dispute resolution**: Heirs have clear guidelines for business interest distribution, reducing conflict.

Steps:

1. Review ownership documents to confirm transferable stakes.
2. Collaborate with legal and financial professionals to restructure ownership for the trust.
3. Update trust provisions with specific plans for business management and succession.

Digital Assets

Digital assets are becoming increasingly important in estate planning. These can include cryptocurrencies, online business accounts, intellectual property, and income-generating social media profiles. Including them in your living trust ensures continuity and access for beneficiaries while safeguarding their value.

Benefits:

- **Protection from loss**: Ensures that critical access details like passwords or private keys are preserved for beneficiaries.
- **Continuity for online ventures**: Facilitates seamless handover of income-generating platforms, such as blogs or e-commerce sites.
- **Legal clarity**: Prevents disputes over ownership and income distribution.

Steps:

1. **Compile an inventory**: List all digital assets, including their descriptions, estimated values, and account credentials.
2. **Document access**: Record usernames, passwords, and security keys securely (e.g., in a digital vault).
3. **Work with an expert**: Consult legal professionals specializing in digital assets to align the trust with emerging regulations.

4. **Outline management plans**: Specify in the trust how assets should be accessed, used, or liquidated by beneficiaries.

5. **Update regularly**: Periodically review the inventory to account for evolving platforms or market values.

Expert Guidance for Complex Transfers

Some assets, such as businesses and high-value investments, require expert input to comply with regulatory requirements and avoid legal challenges. Professionals can guide you through intricate processes, ensuring the trust remains compliant and protected.

Steps:

1. Identify assets with complex transfer requirements.

2. Consult a lawyer or financial advisor specializing in trusts.

3. Execute tailored solutions, such as business restructuring, to incorporate these assets seamlessly.

Once assets are transferred into a living trust, the work of managing them continues. You need to regularly evaluate to ensure that the trust's assets remain aligned with shifting financial landscapes and personal objectives. Proactive management helps maintain the trust's functionality while reducing the need for major restructuring in the future. This involves scheduling periodic reviews of asset performance and alignment with goals, updating the trust to reflect changes such as new acquisitions or market fluctuations, and monitoring documentation to ensure compliance with evolving regulations. Active trust management creates a resilient framework for seamless inheritance, safeguarding assets and allowing beneficiaries to enjoy their intended benefits with clarity and ease.

Transferring Assets into the Trust

Let's discuss some critical steps needed to ensure assets are effectively transferred into a living trust.

Understanding Legal Transfer Processes

Understanding how to transfer assets into a living trust is pivotal for managing those assets effectively. Legal transfer processes vary depending on asset type. Real estate, for instance, requires a deed assignment into the trust's name, typically a deed of trust or a warranty deed. Likewise, bank accounts must often be retitled, and businesses could demand documentation like operating agreements or stock certificates. Understand each asset class's process level, emphasizing that clarity in these legal procedures is essential in preventing missteps that might undermine the trust's enforceability.

Understanding legal procedures builds confidence. Knowing the steps involved gives you a key advantage: reducing the chances of mistakes. Errors or oversights can lead to disputes or even invalidate the transfer of assets. By fully grasping the required steps, from learning important terms to preparing for potential hurdles, you put yourself in a stronger position to manage assets effectively within your trust.

Documenting the Transfers

Thorough documentation is indispensable. It's your insurance policy against potential disputes, serving to protect your interests and validate rightful ownership. Obscure or missing records could fuel disagreements, threatening beneficiaries' claims to assets. Prevent this by compiling and maintaining clear, detailed records of transfers, including any signatures or necessary verifications.

Create a secure system for organizing transfer documents, including deeds, titles, and account forms. Periodically review documentation to ensure alignment with the trust's structure. You also need to provide beneficiaries with access to necessary paperwork during the transition phase. Though labor-intensive, it reassures all parties involved of the transfer's legitimacy and trustworthiness.

Moreover, documenting each step of the process allows for greater transparency and understanding among all parties involved. This documentation should be clear and concise, steering away from ambiguity and fostering transparency. When beneficiaries see a well-documented trail, they gain a sense of assurance that the trustor's intentions are being respected and realized.

Using Change of Title Forms

Crucial to this is the role of the change of title forms. They legally transfer the asset from personal to trust ownership. For vehicles or real property, completing these forms with precision ensures the assets are unmistakably linked to the trust.

Efficient title changes confirm the trust's legal claim, reassuring beneficiaries and cutting red tape when the time for distribution arises. Missteps here can mean delays or even legal challenges, especially in states with stringent transfer laws. Therefore, take care to complete and submit these forms diligently. Specifics vary, often requiring the trustee's signature and sometimes a notary or government official's confirmation.

Consulting Professionals When Necessary

Sometimes, the inherent complexity of certain assets necessitates more than just personal diligence. It demands professional oversight. Real estate with liabilities, portfolios with a mix of taxable and non-taxable accounts, or businesses with multi-layered ownership structures can overwhelm even the most vigilant trustee. Knowing when to seek guidance is half the battle.

State laws can present a lot of requirements and stipulations, each varying significantly. Professionals help manage this situation, ensuring compliance and obviating missteps that might invite financial penalties or legal challenges. Ignorance here is costly. Therefore, align complex transfers with professional insight and safeguard your assets.

Examples abound where professional advice transforms intricate transfers into guarantee-backed processes. Take, for instance, an investment portfolio with embedded gains. Without cautious handling, unsuspecting trustees face tax entanglements. An advisor's input can structure the trust to minimize exposure, advising on ideal transfer timing and exploiting tax laws.

Now that assets are securely housed within the trust, our focus will shift to ongoing asset management. It sets the stage for continuous engagement, underlining effective long-term management strategies.

Administering a living trust doesn't end with asset placement. It's an ongoing, calculated process of monitoring, adjusting, and managing assets as life circumstances shift. Assets' nature changes; some appreciate, others depreciate. Beneficiaries' needs evolve, as might tax implications or income distributions.

Transferring assets into a living trust creates a stable foundation that supports its long-term functionality. The key to effective trust management lies in maintaining a routine of regular reviews and making adjustments to reflect changes in asset value or relevance to your broader financial strategy. Trust management is not solely about adhering to rigid rules but about fostering financial health through thoughtful decisions and strategic planning. Combining asset placement with active oversight ensures that the trust remains a responsive and adaptable tool, capable of meeting evolving needs and objectives effectively. This dynamic approach transforms your living trust into a powerful, living document that grows and adapts alongside your financial goals.

A trust that keeps pace with transformation remains a formidable ally. As you continue this journey, see the next discussions as an opportunity to integrate comprehensive asset oversight into your financial toolkit.

So, gear up for guidance on management strategies that ensure your trust remains as dynamic and effective as the assets it safeguards. Keep the focus on integrating these strategies into a broader narrative of financial wellness and preparedness, aligning tomorrow's needs with today's proactive management strategies.

Ongoing Asset Management

Asset management ensures the vitality and relevance of the trust over time. After understanding the legal steps for asset transfers, it's important to focus on managing those assets effectively. The integrity and objectives of the trust depend heavily on how well these assets are looked after. When we think about managing assets within a living trust, it involves a few key practices: regularly reviewing asset inventory, monitoring performance, and making informed decisions based on that information.

Regularly Reviewing the Asset Inventory

Your trust is like a garden. Just having it laid out beautifully isn't enough. It requires attention and active care. Similarly, your assets require regular attention to ensure they stay aligned with your goals. This is where regular reviews come into play. Keeping your inventory up to date serves as a clear roadmap, reflecting the current state of your assets. This careful tracking ensures beneficiaries won't encounter unexpected surprises later, fostering trust and instilling confidence in the process.

Monitoring Asset Performance

You become better equipped to make smart decisions by understanding how your assets are behaving in the market and how your own financial circumstances might be evolving. This could mean deciding whether to hold onto a certain property or stock or to let it go based on current or anticipated market conditions. For instance, if you notice a particular stock consistently underperforming but have insights indicating potential growth, you might opt to retain it a bit longer. Conversely, if the market signals a downturn, liquidating the asset could be a strategic move.

These notions aren't just theoretical. They have very practical applications. Take John, for instance, who discovered through diligent performance monitoring that one of his long-held investments was steadily losing value. This insight pushed him to liquidate it before it became a financial burden, redirecting those funds into a growing tech stock. Such active management ensures that the trust's assets aren't just stagnant but are continuously optimized.

It's important to note that asset management in a living trust isn't just about preventing problems. It's also about seizing opportunities. Keeping your assets in tune with your goals and the shifting market nurtures growth and adaptability, ensuring that your trust doesn't just endure but flourishes over time. For example, regular checks on assets could reveal new opportunities, such as entering into emerging markets or acquiring more stocks in an expanding industry.

Let's break it down further with a hypothetical family exploration: imagine the Smith family, who originally set up their family trust with a focus on real estate. Over the years, with the help of consistent asset management, they noticed a trend in the tech sector. Recognizing this, they began redirecting some resources towards technology investments, which resulted in significant financial growth for their trust.

Managing Trust Assets Proactively

The actions didn't just come from observations but were built upon informed decisions arising from their understanding of dynamic market conditions linked to their vast knowledge of trust operations. This leads us to the importance of being proactive rather than reactive in managing a trust. Looking at your portfolio periodically helps you see how each asset contributes to the bigger picture.

The key takeaway from these insights is empowerment. Actively engaging with your trust gives you the control to shape it in a way that fulfills your ultimate intentions. This isn't merely about responding to changes or keeping things in order, but anchoring one's legacy with the intention and clarity that withstands the test of time.

The goal is to equip you with the knowledge and strategies that streamline your asset management process, making it both manageable and beneficial. Visualizing this process is step one. The steps to implement it are journey and guideposts for ensuring your trust achieves its potential.

Asset management fosters a strong foundation rooted in careful planning, regular review, and strategic adjustment. It's the modus operandi essential for maintaining the vitality and purpose of your living trust. Each effort placed into effective management reaps benefits for the present and secures a more certain future.

Through these practices, you can ensure that the seeds you've planted grow into a sustaining legacy. Remember, a well-tended trust isn't just a repository of assets but a reflection of foresight and careful stewardship.

Conclusion

Now that we've unpacked the essentials of managing assets within a living trust, we can confidently move forward with creating secure and adaptable estate plans. Recognizing the diverse nature of assets and ensuring they are well-organized and accurately valued equips us to avoid potential conflicts among beneficiaries and adapt to changes as life evolves. This proactive approach ensures that every asset truly serves its purpose in securing your family's financial future. With ongoing attention to detail and regular updates to match evolving circumstances, your trust becomes a resilient tool for preserving your legacy.

In the next chapter, we will focus on the concept of planning for incapacity. We'll explore how tools like living trusts can provide a secure framework for managing your affairs when you're unable to express your wishes.

Asset Inventory Worksheet

Here's a downloadable template to list assets under various categories:

Asset Inventory Worksheet

Here's a downloadable template to list assets under various categories:

Category	Asset Type	Description (Include key features)	Estimated Value	Ownership Details (Name, shared ownership?)	Associated Documentation (Specify type and status)	Condition/Market Status (e.g. appreciating, depreciating. stable)	Notes (special considerations or future plans)
Real Estate	Family home, rental property, farmland	e.g., 3-bedroom home in city; includes mortgage details			Deeds, mortgage statement, property tax records	Appreciating	
Financial accounts	Bank accounts, stocks, bonds, retirement plans	e.g., Mutual funds with 5-year growth, savings account for emergencies			Statements, account forms, beneficiary designations	Stable or High-growth sectors	
Personal Property	Jewelry, antiques, vehicles, collectibles	e.g., Diamond ring with appraisal value, vintage car collection			Appraisals, titles, insurance certificates	Depreciating (e.g., vehicles), Stable for collectibles	

Chapter 6: Planning for Incapacity

It's easy to assume disaster won't strike when you're healthy, active, and living your life without a hitch. But things can suddenly change. Take Linda, for instance. She was a vibrant entrepreneur, always in control of her thriving business. But when an unexpected illness left her incapacitated, her family faced a difficult situation of managing both her personal affairs and business commitments. With no clear plans or directives in place, they were left juggling endless paperwork, legal hoops, and conflicting opinions while trying to honor what they thought she would have wanted.

This brings us to an often-overlooked yet significant part of life preparation: planning for incapacity. We tend to plan our future around sunny days and achievements, but forget about the storms that might hit. When you can no longer voice your choices due to illness or injury, your financial and personal affairs must remain orderly, and your wishes must be clearly known. This chapter explores how strategic planning, like using living trusts, provides a safety net that protects your assets and ensures your intentions are honored even if you can't communicate them yourself. Whether you're managing plenty of resources or just getting by, the goal is to establish a plan that works best for you and your loved ones.

Importance of Incapacity Planning

When we think about future planning, we often envision retirement, vacations, perhaps even legal wills. The truth is, incapacity can strike at any point, due to illness or unexpected injury. Without proper planning, you may leave behind a tangled web of financial and personal affairs harder to manage when you're not at the helm.

A living trust safeguards your estate while allowing you to specify exactly how your affairs are handled and who does the handling. This foresight prevents ambiguity, ensuring your intentions are transparently respected. For example, if you have a particular vision for your healthcare decisions or how financial obligations should be managed, setting those directives in stone now avoids heartache later.

Why Many Avoid the Topic?

Many shy away from incapacity planning due to the discomfort associated with contemplating illness or death. It's an emotional hurdle. Opening the door to these discussions can feel daunting, yet it's a leap worth taking. Facing such intense emotions opens the door to honest and meaningful discussions with family and friends that are essential for thorough incapacity planning. There's a real empowerment in determining your care preferences, rather than leaving that responsibility to others who might execute their own beliefs or assumptions.

To understand the stakes, consider John and Maria. John put off incapacity planning, thinking he'd get to it eventually. Maria, on the other hand, accepted her vulnerability and established a plan while she was still healthy. When an accident, unfortunately, rendered them both incapacitated, Maria's family faced minimal disruption. Her living trust laid out who would take charge of her finances, ensuring bills were paid and investments managed, according to her wishes. John's family faced a different scenario altogether. Without guidance, they struggled to access bank accounts, manage daily expenses, or even agree on decisions related to his care.

Emotional Considerations

Financial interests are only part of the equation, though. Personal wishes, beliefs, and values hold equal weight. No one wants to imagine a scenario where they can't express these, but planning allows you to encode your desires, from simple day-to-day needs to long-term care preferences. Doing so reduces family tensions. Decisions ranging from healthcare options to financial management can easily turn divisive without a clear blueprint. It's one less burden on your loved ones' shoulders, allowing them to focus on support rather than stress.

It's commonplace for people to avoid difficult discussions about potential incapacity, brushing off concerns with, "It won't happen to me," or, "I'll deal with it later." Yet, ignoring these thoughts won't change reality. Bringing them to the surface helps you take charge, turning discomfort into safety and unease into action. It's an act of love and responsibility.

Let's not forget the peace of mind that comes with planning ahead. Knowing your affairs are organized, your preferences specified, and your loved ones positioned to carry out your wishes is comforting. It's like tidying up your life's files for when you might need them most, a win-win for both you and your family.

Living trusts bridge the gap between incapacity and your lucidity, upholding your stated directions. As you shift into understanding the specific mechanics of living trusts, remember the important function they serve in incapacity planning. They form an integral part of ensuring your wishes aren't just hopes, but tangibly enacted realities.

Don't wait until it's too late to plan for incapacity. Open those truthful, if tough, dialogues and take practical steps today. Utilize the opportunity to craft your personal blueprint, one that accompanies you no matter what life throws your way, ensuring continuity and respect for your choices.

How Trusts Can Manage Incapacity?

Planning for incapacity might feel uncomfortable, but it's an essential part of preparing for the future. Starting early allows you to control how your affairs are managed if you become incapable. This not only eases the burden on your family but also ensures that your wishes are carried out precisely as you intend.

Role of Trusts During Incapacity

Living trusts shine as a powerful tool for protecting assets and ensuring seamless financial management during incapacity. Unlike wills that take effect after passing, living trusts operate while you're alive, stepping in seamlessly when you're unable to manage your affairs. They act like a legal blueprint, detailed and customizable, offering you flexibility. You determine who oversees your finances, how you want things managed, and what happens to your assets, all without requiring court intervention.

Think of trusts as autopilots for your financial life. When you're unable to steer, they ensure that your journey stays on course. For instance, a family might face a situation where a parent with dementia can no longer handle financial decisions. A living trust can automatically allow the designated trustee to manage bills, property, and investments according to the parent's wishes. This avoids potential disruptions and ensures continuity in managing assets, preventing family members from having to argue over decisions or seek court directions.

Appointment of Successor Trustees

One of the trust's core components is appointing a successor trustee, a person you rely on to take over if you can't handle your affairs. You need to select someone trustworthy. Consider someone with a sound financial sense, but more importantly, someone who genuinely understands your values and wishes. This person will make significant decisions on your behalf, like distributing funds for care or maintaining property. Having this pre-arranged can lift a considerable weight off your family's shoulders, streamlining transitions during difficult times. It prevents potential family disputes by laying out a clear plan on who manages your affairs, reducing the risk of legal complications .

Avoiding Court Interventions

Securing a living trust allows you to avoid the cumbersome process of legal guardianship. Guardianship can involve lengthy and costly court procedures, requiring family members to prove your incapacity and the appointment of someone to act on your behalf, which is often laden with bureaucratic hurdles. Trusts, on the other hand, bypass this need entirely. For example, a woman who became temporarily incapacitated after an accident could have her pre-appointed trustee step in to manage her business and personal finances, avoiding unnecessary court battles and allowing her family to focus on her recovery.

Flexibility of Trusts

Flexibility is one of the defining features of living trusts. They aren't set in stone and can change as your life does. Maybe your health care preferences evolve, or there's a significant change in your family, like a divorce or new marriage. Trusts accommodate these shifts. Real-life instances highlight situations where people have amended their trusts to provide for new family members or adjusted distributions due to changes in personal convictions. This adaptability ensures that the trust continues to reflect your wishes and circumstances, even as they change.

Think of living trusts and powers of attorney (POA) as partners in planning. While trusts manage your assets, POAs address other essential aspects of decision-making, such as appointing someone to make health decisions or manage day-to-day personal matters. Combining both provides a comprehensive approach to incapacity planning, covering all bases so that no aspect of your life is left without a safety net.

This blend of assets and personal decision-making ensures you're protected on all fronts. Without it, families often find themselves in court disputes, fighting over who should make decisions, or confused about managing daily necessities alongside financial ones. With both structures in place, there's a solid roadmap, offering peace of mind and saving time, money, and emotional energy.

As we move forward, we'll discuss how power of attorney plays into this broader strategy. Whereas trusts look after your financial path, POAs step in to cover personal affairs, making sure someone you trust manages challenges in a way you approve. Each tool complements the other, ensuring that, should the unforeseen happen, every aspect of your life is managed as you desire. With such plans, you're preparing for incapacity while ensuring a legacy that reflects your values, keeps your loved ones secure, and offers peace of mind in knowing everything has been thoughtfully arranged.

Choosing a Power of Attorney

While trusts manage assets, they don't address all decision-making needs, especially in situations that demand immediate action or go beyond financial concerns. Here, the power of attorney (POA) steps in as a significant complement to this structure. A POA provides authority to a trusted individual to make decisions on behalf of the incapacitated person, covering gaps the living trust alone might not fill.

Selecting a Trusted Agent

Choosing the right POA is paramount. By doing so, you're ensuring your values and wishes are upheld by someone capable and aligned with your vision. The selected agent should be someone you trust implicitly to manage an array of responsibilities, from financial tasks like managing investments to making important life choices about medical care when necessary. A POA is not just about assigning duties. You're putting your interests in capable hands, ensuring peace of mind when life's uncertainties arise.

Consider, for example, the story of Emily, who appointed her brother as her POA due to his financial savvy and understanding of her health concerns. Emily took time to communicate her expectations clearly, outlining her financial thresholds, her preferences for care facilities should the need arise, and her emotional considerations regarding family members. This comprehensive approach ensured that her brother understood her stance and was prepared to act accordingly. Emily's meticulous preparation allowed her to face uncertain times confidently, knowing her wishes would be respected and her interests safeguarded.

Such careful selection helps in mitigating potential conflicts, both expected and unforeseen. Think of a situation where siblings with conflicting opinions about an ailing parent's care, unable to make decisions due to the lack of clear documentation or an established decision-making process. This situation can result in emotional conflicts and an inability to move forward with important choices. Having a designated POA allows trusted family members to focus on shared goals, minimizing the chances of friction or misunderstandings.

Communicating Your Wishes

Effective communication between the appointee and the appointed is essential for successfully managing the responsibilities. Engaging in open dialogue ensures everyone is on the same page and aware of the granular details of the POA's authority. This does not mean dictating your terms. The focus should be on fostering a shared understanding of scenarios and responses. This includes having honest discussions about priorities and revisiting these conversations periodically to address shifts in personal circumstances or legal frameworks that may affect decision-making.

Updating POA Documents

As much as initial communication is necessary, regular reviews of POA documents are equally important. This ensures that all considerations remain relevant over time. Life is dynamic as relationships change, and new legal precedents can alter previous understandings. Aligning your POA with these changing variables minimizes the risk of outdated instructions leading to unforeseen complications. For instance, a once-trusted business partner might no longer hold the same influence in your life, necessitating a change in your POA designation.

The process of choosing a POA should also include a detailed examination and discussion about written directives. These directives can guide the POA's actions, such as instructing them on the level of aggressiveness in medical treatments or specifying financial divestment strategies. Adopting a transparent approach when developing these directives minimizes the likelihood of ambiguities that can leave your wishes unfulfilled due to misinterpretation, especially in high-pressure moments when calm, clear decision-making is critical.

The practicalities involved in these preparations often go beyond the mere formalization of intentions. Engaging with a legal expert can provide clarity, ensuring all documents meet necessary legal requirements and addressing questions that might not be obvious to someone without a legal background. Legal expertise can also shed light on complex issues like tax implications and interstate recognition of POA documents, equipping you with essential tools to navigate the intricacies of incapacity planning with an informed perspective.

Once the decision-making structures are established, your thoughts might naturally extend beyond the scope of the POA. Having addressed who will make decisions on your behalf, it's wise to consider what decisions you wish them to make, particularly concerning medical care. Moving on to health care directives and living wills introduces the significant task of detailing your care preferences. These instruments ensure that your medical treatment is according to your wishes, offering reassurance that even the most personal decisions honor your desires.

In sum, navigating the decision-making landscape of incapacity involves more than simply identifying a trusted agent. It requires an ongoing, proactive approach to maintaining alignment with personal desires and legal requirements. The evolution of human relationships and priorities demands regular appraisal, ensuring that each choice steadfastly reflects current realities. Implementing these strategies strengthens resilience and ensures continuity in your life plan, helping you approach future challenges with determination and clarity.

Health Care Directives and Living Wills

Planning for medical care in situations where communication may not be possible is an essential step to ensure your preferences are respected. Health care directives and living wills are powerful tools that help articulate your choices clearly and alleviate potential challenges for loved ones.

Understanding Health Care Directives

Health care directives are legal documents that outline medical treatment preferences in scenarios where individuals are unable to express their decisions. These directives provide clarity to medical professionals and family members, ensuring that your care aligns with your values and desires.

Having specific instructions reduces ambiguity, making it easier for family members and medical teams to follow your predetermined wishes. When decisions are documented in advance, loved ones are spared the stress of guessing or debating over what you might have wanted during critical moments.

For example, health care directives can specify whether you prefer aggressive treatments in life-threatening situations or wish to avoid interventions that may prolong suffering. These clear guidelines can prevent emotional conflicts among family members and facilitate smoother decision-making processes.

Creating a Living Will

A living will focuses on end-of-life care preferences and acts as a guide for difficult medical decisions. This document empowers you to communicate what treatments you do or do not want in scenarios involving serious health crises.

Establishing a living will opens up valuable conversations with loved ones about sensitive topics. It allows you to express your views on life-sustaining measures, such as resuscitation, intubation, and artificial nutrition. This transparency provides peace of mind, as your preferences are clearly communicated and understood.

In addition to offering clarity to medical professionals and family members, a living will also serves as a reflection of your values related to health and dignity. For instance, someone who prioritizes a natural end-of-life experience may specify that they wish to avoid invasive procedures aimed at prolonging life. Such decisions, thoughtfully documented, can relieve loved ones from the burden of making emotionally charged choices during difficult times.

The Role of Medical Agents

Health care directives often involve assigning a medical agent, also known as a health care proxy, who serves as a representative to advocate for your medical preferences. This individual plays a key role in bridging the gap between your documented wishes and real-time decision-making during critical situations.

Medical agents act as spokespersons, ensuring that your decisions are upheld even when circumstances become complex. For example, in cases where treatments or procedures require nuanced judgment, a medical agent can interpret your wishes and communicate them effectively to healthcare providers.

Choosing a trusted individual as your medical agent provides reassurance that someone who understands your values will guide the decision-making process. This reduces potential burdens for family members, as the appointed agent takes on the responsibility of ensuring your preferences are respected.

Importance of Regular Reviews

Health care directives and living wills are not static documents. They should be revisited periodically to ensure that they remain aligned with your current values and circumstances. Regular reviews are essential to keep your instructions up to date with changes in your health, family dynamics, or personal outlook.

Updating these documents ensures their accuracy and relevance, which is especially important if your preferences evolve over time. For example, a shift in perspective regarding life-sustaining measures or advancements in medical technologies may lead you to reconsider previous choices.

Sharing updates with family members and medical agents keeps everyone informed and minimizes potential tensions. When loved ones are familiar with your preferences, they can act with greater confidence and unity in situations requiring critical decisions.

Health care directives and living wills are indispensable tools for expressing your medical wishes clearly when you can no longer communicate them yourself. They provide guidance for loved ones and medical professionals, helping to prevent confusion and emotional conflicts during challenging times.

Understanding health care directives, creating a living will, assigning a medical agent, and regularly reviewing your plans ensure that your choices remain respected and relevant. These documents represent an important step in empowering individuals to maintain control over their medical care, fostering peace of mind for both themselves and their families.

Conclusion

Preparing for potential incapacity through living trust strategies highlights the value of taking control of our future. This chapter has emphasized the importance of safeguarding our intentions and alleviating stress for loved ones during difficult times. Living trusts provide a reliable solution for managing assets and ensuring that financial matters are handled efficiently, without unnecessary legal challenges. Proactive planning allows us to face uncertainties with confidence and ensures that our wishes are honored. As we wrap up this discussion, it's clear that these tools are not just practical measures but acts of care and responsibility for ourselves and those we hold dear. Now is the time to turn understanding into action and take meaningful steps toward securing peace of mind and stability.

In the next chapter, we will discuss the responsibilities of trustees, offering insights into their duties, legal obligations, and strategies for effectively managing trust assets.

Chapter 7: Legal and Financial Considerations

Estate planning can often feel daunting. It requires navigating a complex landscape of legal requirements and financial details. One significant hurdle is grasping the intricacies of living trusts. Designed to provide security and simplicity, these instruments accompany a range of complicated legal and financial factors that can easily overwhelm anyone.

You might have plenty of questions. How do taxes impact a living trust compared to a simple will? What responsibilities do trustees bear, and how does one minimize costs while maximizing benefits? These are just a few of the issues we'll answer as we explore the legal and financial layers tied to living trusts. Our goal is to provide clarity and guidance, helping you move forward with confidence in your estate planning journey.

Tax Implications of Living Trusts

Taxes might not be the most thrilling topic, but they're imperative when it comes to living trusts. Understanding taxes helps you make informed decisions in estate planning. Let's break this down by first looking at the tax types that affect living trusts, along with income and estate taxes, comparing them to how wills are taxed.

Understanding Tax Types

Living trusts mainly encounter two types of taxes: income taxes and estate taxes. The trustee of a living trust is responsible for reporting any income generated by trust assets. This is similar to filing your personal income taxes. However, there's a twist. If you place assets in a living trust, those assets might still be considered part of your estate upon passing. This distinction could have consequences for estate taxes.

Estate taxes are levied on the total value of your estate - every asset you leave behind. When it comes to wills, estate taxes automatically apply at death. But with living trusts, the situation gets a bit more complex. Assets within a properly funded living trust might avoid probate, which can mean potential tax advantages if structured effectively.

When we talk about the tax advantages of living trusts, one standout is avoiding the probate process, which can be time-consuming and expensive. Eliminating probate can potentially reduce the income and estate tax burdens on beneficiaries because assets transfer seamlessly. However, the benefits depend on how well the trust is funded. Proper funding refers to the allocation of assets into the trust during your lifetime, ensuring the intended tax efficiencies.

Tax Strategies

Let's understand some strategies.

- **The order of asset distribution:** Distributing taxable accounts in a specific order can help reduce the overall tax burden, instead of simply dividing them evenly among beneficiaries. Thoughtful planning in asset distribution can lead to significant savings.

- **Consult a tax professional:** A tax expert can provide tailored strategies that align with your unique situation. Their expertise ensures that your decisions are informed and optimized to minimize tax liabilities effectively.

- **Utilize deductions and exclusions:** Clear planning can help beneficiaries tap into deductions and exclusions that provide substantial tax relief. For example, deductions tied to trust management expenses, medical costs, mortgage interests, or charitable donations can significantly lower taxable income when accounted for properly.

Joe, a hypothetical trust beneficiary, faced uncertainty about managing assets inherited from a living trust. After consulting with a tax expert, he discovered how deductions on trust-related expenses could reduce his tax liability. For Joe, medical expenses, charitable donations, and mortgage interest connected to the trust offered considerable financial relief. This example highlights the importance of consulting professionals and developing a clear plan to optimize benefits.

Tax Reporting Responsibilities

An often overlooked area is tax reporting responsibilities. You need to know how to report any income the trust earns. Accurate record-keeping is your best friend here. Every transaction, expense, and change needs documentation, not just for the moment but for any potential future audits.

With living trusts, income is generally reported on either Form 1040 or 1041, depending on who receives the income and whether the trust is revocable or irrevocable. Filing deadlines and requirements are strict. Missing these can lead to penalties for non-compliance, potentially eroding the very tax advantages you sought to gain by creating the trust. A proactive stance in filing ensures compliance and prevents unexpected liabilities.

Future Tax Change

While current tax laws shape how trusts are managed today, keeping an eye on future changes is equally important. Tax laws can evolve with political and economic shifts, affecting estate tax thresholds or altering how trusts themselves are treated. Discussions about the estate tax have been buzzing for years, with varying thresholds impacting whether estates are taxed and at what rate.

Anticipating shifts in legislation helps you make proactive decisions. Suppose the estate tax threshold was lowered. Trusts currently untaxed might suddenly face liabilities. By planning for such scenarios, perhaps through alternative investments or by adjusting the beneficiaries' distribution plans, you can mitigate the impact of these changes.

Strategizing for the future goes beyond just protecting against change and involves actively pursuing potential new opportunities. For instance, if laws favor smaller estates, consider splitting trusts into smaller segments to capitalize on these benefits.

Finally, let's transition smoothly to the forthcoming section on trustee responsibilities by spotlighting how managing tax roles interlinks with trustee duties. The trustee isn't just an asset manager; they are the linchpin in maintaining tax compliance. Grasping tax duties eases this responsibility significantly. A trustee well-versed in taxes can liaise efficiently with professionals, foresee potential issues before they arise, and ensure the trust functions optimally for beneficiaries.

This clear understanding of taxes underscores the broader trustee role. While legal duties might primarily focus on asset management, the financial aspect is equally vital. A trustee who melds these responsibilities can maintain the trust's integrity, ensuring it serves its intended purpose while respecting both the grantor's intentions and the beneficiaries' needs.

Consider this—you've now got a solid foundation to dive deeper into the intertwining responsibilities of trustees, complementing the tax knowledge we've uncovered. This understanding helps you not only now but also provides a framework for navigating future obligations, making the vast world of estate planning just a bit less daunting. So, as we look ahead, grasp the connection between taxes and trusteeship; they're two sides of the same coin that ensure your estate plan stands firm.

Trustee Responsibilities and Duties

Understanding the responsibilities of a trustee is essential for managing a trust effectively. Trustees hold an important role in ensuring the trust operates as intended and serves the best interests of the beneficiaries. This section explores the key aspects of a trustee's role in detail.

Duties of a Trustee

Trustees are responsible for executing their duties ethically and impartially. Maintaining transparency in their actions ensures trust between the trustee and beneficiaries.

- **Ethical obligations**: Trustees act as fiduciaries, meaning they are legally and ethically bound to act in the best interests of the beneficiaries. Their decisions must reflect integrity and adherence to the trust's terms.
- **Impartial decision-making**: Trustees must avoid favoritism and ensure that all beneficiaries are treated fairly. Decisions regarding the management of assets should prioritize the trust's objectives over personal biases.
- **Communication and transparency**: Establishing open communication with beneficiaries is critical. Sharing updates about the trust's status, financial performance, and any major decisions fosters a sense of accountability and trustworthiness.

Managing Trust Assets

Effective administration of the trust's assets is one of the primary responsibilities of a trustee. Trustees are required to invest trust assets responsibly, striking a balance between the beneficiaries' immediate needs and long-term financial security. Accurate financial records must be maintained, and regular updates provided to beneficiaries, ensuring transparency and demonstrating appropriate management. Failure to manage assets appropriately can lead to financial losses, legal disputes, or even the collapse of the trust, highlighting the critical nature of this responsibility.

Legal Compliance

Adhering to legal requirements is crucial for trustees to ensure the validity and functionality of the trust. Trustees must fulfill their fiduciary responsibilities diligently, as breaches can result in legal action from beneficiaries and damage the trust's integrity. Completing necessary legal filings, such as annual accounts or tax returns, is essential to comply with relevant state and federal regulations. Staying organized and consulting legal professionals when necessary helps trustees avoid non-compliance, which could lead to financial penalties or legal consequences.

The role of a trustee involves significant responsibilities, requiring ethical conduct, financial expertise, and strict legal compliance. Understanding these aspects helps in selecting the right trustee and ensuring the trust is managed effectively. A well-informed trustee, supported by a structured management plan, contributes to the successful administration of the trust and lasting benefits for the beneficiaries.

Costs Associated with Establishing a Trust

Understanding the financial landscape of living trusts is important for anyone involved in estate planning or dealing with trustee responsibilities. Just as trustees must grasp their duties, they also need to be aware of the initial and ongoing costs that come with setting up and maintaining a living trust. These financial aspects are integral, influencing the sustainability of a trust and its effectiveness as an estate planning tool.

Initial Costs

The up-front costs of creating a living trust can vary widely, affected by factors such as complexity, attorney fees, and state laws. Unlike a simple will, which might pass through probate, a living trust can sidestep this process, but this benefit involves higher initial expenses.

- **Attorney fees**: Professional guidance is essential for drafting the trust correctly, ensuring all legal requirements are met, and minimizing the risk of complications later on.

- **Costs for documentation or consultations**: Additional expenses may arise for obtaining necessary documentation or scheduling extra legal consultations, especially for estates with complex assets or unusual stipulations.

- **Importance of comparing quotes**: Obtaining multiple quotes from different service providers allows for a thorough comparison of services and fees, helping to avoid overspending.

- **Package deals from attorneys**: Some attorneys offer estate planning package deals that include related documents, such as power of attorney or advance healthcare directives, potentially saving money in the long run.

- **Hidden fees**: Administrative costs, such as document storage or making amendments to the trust over time, often catch people by surprise. Identifying these potential hidden expenses upfront can prevent unexpected adjustments and save money.

Ongoing Costs

Shifting to ongoing costs, the financial responsibilities continue well after the trust is established. Regular financial reporting and compliance with tax obligations are essential. Trustees often require tools and professional services to ensure these tasks are completed accurately and efficiently. Accounting fees can add up, especially if the trust is complex and involves multiple beneficiaries or income streams. Legal audits may be needed periodically, particularly if the estate's value fluctuates or if there are substantial changes in tax laws.

Cost-Saving Strategies

Strategies for minimizing ongoing expenses are varied and can significantly impact the financial burden.

- **Utilize self-help resources**: Use kits and online templates to draft and fund your trust, reducing initial expenses while avoiding errors.
- **Streamline administrative tasks**: Assign roles within the family to share responsibilities effectively and save on professional fees.
- **Leverage digital tools**: Use technology to monitor assets efficiently and reduce manual oversight through automation.

When comparing living trusts to other estate planning options, the cost-effectiveness becomes more apparent. Traditional wills will often entail lower initial costs but incur expenses during probate. Probate fees can be a substantial downside, coupled with the lengthy duration of the process. In contrast, a living trust, despite higher upfront expenses, can result in considerable savings by avoiding probate altogether. This aspect alone is persuasive for many, reducing stress and uncertainty for beneficiaries.

For example, consider an estate valued at $500,000. If settled through probate, costs can be around $10,000 in fees alone, not to mention the time delay, which can extend for months. A living trust, while potentially costing $3,000 to set up, bypasses probate, providing quicker asset distribution and privacy for beneficiaries.

Understanding these financial commitments involves not only assessing costs but also recognizing the financial benefits of these trusts over time. Savings from probate avoidance are just one aspect. Reduced administrative burdens and potentially lower tax liabilities over the years significantly add to their appeal.

It is essential to consider the legal aspects, which offer protective measures that further enhance a living trust's value. Legal safeguards, such as protection from creditors and clear stipulations for incapacity, provide peace of mind. Recognizing the intersection between managing costs and these protective features is key to appreciating how living trusts can serve as a powerful estate planning tool.

In the upcoming section, we will discuss these legal protections, providing a comprehensive view of the peace and control that living trusts afford you, alongside financial prudence. Understanding both sides of the coin, financial and legal, will enable you to make informed choices about estate planning, ensuring that a living trust meets both current and future needs.

Legal Protections Afforded by Living Trusts

In considering living trusts, the earlier section on financial implications laid out the costs tied to setting one up. However, these expenses contribute to essential legal safeguards that are among the key benefits of living trusts. It's a strategy that not only preserves finances but ensures your assets face fewer risks, amplifying its value in robust estate planning.

Asset Protection

One key area is asset protection. Living trusts may protect your assets from creditors, insulating them by keeping ownership at arm's length. However, this isn't foolproof across all legal contexts. For instance, irrevocable trusts tend to offer stronger creditor protection compared to revocable trusts, which permit the grantor to retain control and thus expose assets to liability. Compared to other protection tools like LLCs, living trusts can offer more personal asset coverage if structured shrewdly. Assets placed in a properly managed trust can be less susceptible to claims, but consulting a legal professional is critical since the effectiveness varies with state laws and trust structuring specifics.

Privacy Assurance

The privacy a living trust confers distinguishes it from a will, which undergoes public probate processes. This privacy prevents public exposure of financial details, sidestepping potential family discord that can arise with such revelations. Take, for example, a trust designed to quietly distribute significant assets to a family member struggling with debt. Privacy ensures these sensitive distributions don't spark quarrels or jealousy that might fracture family ties. Knowing your plan remains unknown to those outside it can offer peace in the distribution process, leaving fewer chances for disputes.

Simplified Access for Beneficiaries

Beneficiaries also enjoy improved access to their inheritances through reduced probate procedures. Living trusts streamline transitions, passing assets directly without delays characteristic of probate. This efficiency minimizes both time and costs, often yielding smoother pathways for beneficiaries. Consider heirs who gain access to finances promptly, sparing them the cash flow issues they might otherwise face while mired in lengthy legal proceedings. This simplification means assets aren't held in limbo but move as intended, reinforcing the trust's worth in estate planning.

For heightened clarity, envision a simple example: a grandparent planning for their grandchildren's future. By setting a living trust, they ensure grandchildren receive funds directly for education or other needs without probate roadblocks, maintaining the intention and timing critical to such plans. This preemptive approach upholds their legacy through a smooth, intentional asset transfer process.

As we gather these observations, it's clear that each element of a living trust functions together in safeguarding assets and maintaining control. Privacy, for instance, is not only about secrecy but ties directly into preventing family rifts and protecting sensitive bequests. Asset protection not only repels creditors but intersects significantly with how beneficiaries receive their designated shares.

Conclusion

The legal protections afforded by living trusts offer significant advantages that go beyond financial benefits. They provide a robust framework for safeguarding assets, ensuring privacy, and preparing for unexpected situations such as incapacity. These trusts also simplify the transfer of assets to beneficiaries, eliminating many of the delays and complexities associated with probate. Understanding these legal advantages enhances your appreciation of how living trusts serve as a crucial instrument in estate planning, providing both protection and reassurance for you and your beneficiaries.

In the next chapter, we'll debunk common myths about living trusts, ensuring clarity on their true purpose and benefits.

Interactive Scenario: Structuring a Living Trust for Legal Protections

Imagine this situation:

Alex wants to create a living trust to ensure assets are protected from creditors while maintaining privacy for the family. The estate includes a vacation property, a small business, and savings in multiple accounts. Additionally, Alex wishes to provide for children in a way that avoids family disputes. How should Alex structure the trust to achieve these goals?

1. **What type of trust would work best for Alex?**
   1. Revocable Trust

   2. Irrevocable Trust

      Explanation: An irrevocable trust offers stronger creditor protection, as assets are no longer directly owned by Alex. A revocable trust provides more flexibility but may expose assets to liability.

2. **Which assets should Alex include in the trust?**
   1. Only the vacation property and business

   2. All assets, including savings accounts

      Explanation: Including all assets ensures comprehensive protection, but funding the trust appropriately is critical for its effectiveness.

3. **Who should serve as trustee for maximum privacy?**
   1. A trusted family member

   2. A professional trustee

      Explanation: A professional trustee can ensure impartial management and maintain confidentiality, while a family member might bring familiarity but could lead to disputes if roles are not clearly defined.

4. **How can Alex prepare for potential incapacity?**
   1. Select a clear successor trustee and document responsibilities

2. Skip planning for incapacity

   Explanation: Preparing for incapacity ensures the trust is managed seamlessly without court involvement, protecting assets and maintaining stability.

Outcome feedback: Choosing an irrevocable trust, including all assets, appointing a professional trustee, and planning for incapacity provides Alex with robust creditor protection, privacy, and effective trust management. These decisions align with the goal of ensuring a secure and well-structured living trust.

Chapter 8: Common Misconceptions About Living Trusts

Think about Tom, who always believed that living trusts were strictly for the ultra-wealthy. When his friend Mike shared how a living trust had smoothed the transition of his modest estate to his kids, Tom was taken aback. He realized he'd been holding onto misconceptions that stopped him from considering options that might have worked in his favor. Like many, he thought such arrangements only made sense if you owned lavish properties or had a massive fortune. But now, faced with the responsibility of planning his own estate, Tom questioned what he really knew about living trusts and whether he'd let the wrong ideas steer his decisions.

Tom isn't alone. Many people find themselves tangled in myths about living trusts, believing they're unnecessary, too costly, or overly complex if you're not part of the wealthy elite. In this chapter, we'll unravel these common misunderstandings by digging into the real purpose and benefits of living trusts. We aim to offer clarity and insight so that individuals like Tom can make well-informed choices about their financial future and safeguard their legacies.

Addressing the Misconception that Living Trusts Are Only for the Wealthy

Many folks think these trusts only apply to people with sprawling estates or extensive property portfolios. In reality, living trusts represent an inclusive strategy, important for folks at all income levels. They're not just about who gets the family mansion. The trust's focus is on simplifying asset transfers and securing peace of mind for everyone, whether you're passing down a diamond ring or a modest savings account.

Trusts for Average Families

Every family holds a legacy, and it deserves protection. When it comes to distribution, living trusts streamline the process, preventing those tricky legal complications that can arise with wills. If you plan to leave a cherished home or nostalgic possessions to your loved ones, failing to establish proper arrangements can result in court proceedings or family disputes. Such complications are time-consuming and also strain relationships, leaving your loved ones caught in challenging and emotional situations. To avoid these outcomes, creating a living trust becomes a vital step. This document clearly specifies your wishes, ensuring that your desires are upheld seamlessly and without contention. Through a living trust, you provide clarity and security, enabling a smooth transition of your assets and eliminating unnecessary hurdles for your family.

Accessibility to Resources

Accessibility is key. It's easy to assume that setting up a living trust will drain your bank account. Rest assured, that's not the case. Lawyers can help for sure, but they're not the only option. These days, DIY templates with step-by-step guidance make it affordable and straightforward. You'll find many community workshops offer assistance too. They break down the process, ensuring you're not left in the dark. Legal aid organizations, often free of charge or at a lower cost, provide another avenue, making living trusts achievable for any budget.

The Cost of Not Having a Trust

Skipping a living trust has its pitfalls. Without it, estate distribution typically goes through probate, a potentially expensive and certainly time-consuming process. While some might think wills are enough, probate could take up a sizeable chunk of the estate's value due to court fees and administrative costs. It's not uncommon for assets in probate to take months, sometimes years, to reach the rightful heirs. For a family that heavily relies on the timely transfer of assets, this delay can result in financial strain.

Real-Life Examples

Think of Jane, a schoolteacher with a modest estate. She opted for a living trust to leave her children a modest inheritance. When Jane passed, her family accessed their assets promptly. What would have required prolonged legal proceedings was resolved with little more than presenting a certificate of trust. Then there's Tom, whose small business was at the heart of his estate. He used a living trust to ensure a smoother transition of ownership to his children, reducing family stress and preserving the business's value. With a living trust in place, these examples highlight not only cost savings but also how a little foresight can simplify complexities, bringing comfort in a time of loss.

The last thing you want for your family is added worry during an already challenging time. From avoiding high probate fees to preserving relationships, living trusts support your loved ones. Making deliberate choices involves considerations that reach far beyond mere possessions. Consider, for instance, the Beckers, a family of five, who set up a simple living trust to handle their modest estate, including a small savings account, the family car, and a piece of land. When Mr. Becker passed away, the family recognized just how smooth the process had become, no fighting, no confusion, just the assurance that their husband and father's wishes were being honored.

While exploring the breadth of benefits living trusts offer, consider the prospects of not having one. Confusion over asset distribution often ignites disputes, sometimes among siblings who you thought got along just fine. When emotions run high after a loved one passes, avoiding these painful scenarios is invaluable.

A living trust offers the comforting assurance that your family's future is protected, bringing invaluable peace of mind. We're talking about offering security to your loved ones and a clear path that aligns with your wishes. It's a heartening guarantee that what you worked for finds its way to those who matter most without unnecessary detours.

Living trusts serve as a testament to proactive decision-making, available to all, not just the wealthy elite. Everybody deserves the advantage of a seamless transition. Whether you're passing down lifelong savings, a business, or cherished belongings, living trusts stand out as a tool for responsible, caring planning. Taking these steps highlights the importance you place on your family's future and demonstrates your thoughtful approach to addressing every detail with care.

Dispelling the Misunderstanding that Living Trusts Eliminate All Tax Liabilities

Living trusts can offer great flexibility and potential savings in estate planning, a point we touched on in the previous section. They make financial sense for many families, but it's important to dispel the myth that they magically erase all tax concerns.

Tax Responsibilities Remain

Now, let's understand the reality of taxes with living trusts. One common assumption is that placing assets in a living trust shields them completely from all taxes, which simply isn't true. Yes, trusts can offer certain tax efficiencies, but the trust itself isn't a tax-exempt entity. In fact, you remain connected to those tax obligations intricately. If anything, living trusts help in better organizing your commitments rather than eliminating them.

Take, for example, income generated within the trust. Suppose your living trust holds stocks or a rental property. The dividends from those stocks or income from the property don't just vanish from tax assessments. Instead, the trust incurs regular income taxes on these earnings. In most cases, since you, as the grantor, have control over the trust and may even pull income from these resources, you're responsible for reporting this income on your personal tax return.

Consider the larger picture of estate taxes, too. For smaller estates, a living trust is a straightforward mechanism to pass on wealth, but when dealing with sizable estates, the trust doesn't necessarily cushion you from estate taxes. The federal estate tax applies if the value of your estate exceeds a certain threshold, something to watch out for if you've amassed significant assets. Always remember, it's not just what you earn that can be subject to taxes, but also what you leave behind.

Let's examine a hypothetical scenario to bring these ideas to life. Imagine you set up a living trust with investments totaling $1 million, including some lucrative stocks. Over a year, the investments appreciate and return $50,000 in dividends. That's definitely a success, but there's a catch. The IRS wants its share of that success, and you'll need to report this $50,000 on your income tax return. You're not escaping tax duty, but you're better prepared because everything's organized neatly within the trust.

Potential Tax Benefits

Now, what about reducing these tax liabilities? Smart planning can mitigate some of the burdens. For instance, consider strategic gifting. By gifting portions of your estate each year, you systematically reduce the estate's taxable size. The current tax laws allow you to gift a certain amount annually to individuals without triggering gift taxes. Over time, this can significantly lessen the estate's overall taxable value.

Another tactic involves planned distributions to the trust's beneficiaries. Sometimes, distributing income can shift tax liabilities decisively. Maybe there's a family member in a lower tax bracket than you. You can distribute trust income to them, thus lessening your tax burden while still benefiting your family as a whole. It's a bit like playing income management chess with the IRS as your opponent.

Understanding Tax Obligations

Nonetheless, it's important to guide your strategies with professional advice. Tax laws and limits can shift with legislative changes, and staying updated ensures your strategies remain effective. Consulting with a tax professional or attorney is a wise move when dealing with complex financial webs like living trusts. They ensure you comply with current laws while making the most of tax-efficient strategies.

Common Misconceptions Addressed

The misconception that living trusts magically wipe out tax responsibilities stems from a misunderstanding of their purpose and mechanics. Consider them a tool to streamline finances and manage taxes responsibly rather than avoid them. They enhance control, often reduce skepticism in transferring assets, and offer privacy advantages, but they require diligent tax attention.

Moving forward, it's wise to think of trust management as an ongoing responsibility rather than a set-and-forget situation. You've seen how living trusts relate to financial responsibilities. They can help with planning, but they also need careful management.

Living trusts are incredibly effective tools, but their real strength lies in how well they're managed. A clear understanding of your tax obligations is key to using this tool effectively and securing your family's future. Staying informed and planning strategically allow you to ensure your financial intentions are carried out as you envision. Think of this as creating a well-rounded financial plan where living trusts become a central part of achieving your estate planning goals.

Next up, we will explore how deploying additional tools can simplify the process, simplifying complexities surrounding trust management. Innovations in technology and resources are here to bridge gaps, making the once-daunting task of trust administration approachable and straightforward. Being proactive in personal education empowers you to leverage your trust fully and effectively.

Reducing Fears About Trust Complexity

Navigating the complexities of living trusts can feel overwhelming at first, but let's build on the insights we've already covered. We've explored both the advantages and the challenges of living trusts, especially when it comes to tax responsibilities. Now, let's use that foundation to clear up common misconceptions and focus on practical, straightforward ways to approach setting them up.

Simplified Processes

Living trusts are often seen as complicated, largely because they are unfamiliar to many people. This assumption can make the process seem intimidating. However, creating a living trust can be straightforward and manageable with the right approach.

Step-by-step guides available online are designed to assist individuals who have no legal background. These guides provide clear instructions and templates, breaking the process into simple, easy-to-follow tasks. Approaching the process systematically allows even the more detailed aspects of trust creation to become easier to manage.

Consider Sarah, who once faced the same intimidation. She believed she'd need extensive legal coaching and endless resources. However, she discovered user-friendly resources that guided her every step of the way. Sarah's journey began with a reputable workbook that broke down the legal jargon into plain English. Following it allowed her to craft a basic living trust without the need for constant legal intervention. Her story echoes many others who have transitioned into trust management with less friction than anticipated.

Supportive Resources Available

Several online platforms offer free or low-cost courses designed to navigate the ins and outs of setting up a living trust. These can often be completed at your own pace, making them perfect for those with tight schedules. Platforms like Nolo, LegalZoom, and Trust & Will provide accessible tools and resources, including step-by-step guidance and templates, to simplify the process for individuals without a legal background. Community workshops also provide support, where you can engage with individuals in similar situations, learning together and exchanging insights. This environment fosters confidence, turning what might seem a lonely quest into a shared journey.

Moreover, professional guidance remains at hand for those who prefer it. Estate planning specialists often provide consultations that can be beneficial without taking over the entire process. This guidance ensures that if any complexities arise, they are sorted with professional insight, but still keeps you in the driver's seat.

To offer another testament, let's observe how John worked through his trust setup. Initially, overwhelmed by the expectation to depend solely on legal expertise, he discovered an interactive webinar hosted by estate planning professionals. This online seminar broke down each phase of trust creation, while fielding live questions. By the end, John was empowered to draft and manage his trust, reaching out only occasionally for professional advice.

Busting the Complexity Myth

A prevalent myth suggests that only lawyers should handle trusts. However, many individuals have effectively managed to dispel this belief by setting up trusts independently. Taking control of their understanding of trust management enables them to recognize that gradual learning is both achievable and advantageous. This serves as an immense confidence booster and instills a sense of ownership over their estate planning process.

As we look at these examples, it's clear that the layers of complexity perceived around living trusts often dissipate once approached with the right resources and mindset. Understanding this process with the right tools and a proactive approach allows you to navigate it effectively and with ease.

In essence, understanding and dispelling these myths with tangible support can turn the intimidation of living trusts into empowerment. When supported by designed tools, engaging community ecosystems, and occasional professional touches, managing a living trust becomes not just a destination, but an achievable journey.

Before we move to the next part of our exploration, a mention of one more feature of living trusts could be useful. They are exceptionally flexible. You can update or even revoke these trusts as life circumstances evolve. This inherent adaptability serves as the perfect segue into the following discussion, where we'll discuss how these dynamic instruments can adjust alongside your life's changing course.

Clarifying the Myth That Trusts Cannot Be Altered

In our previous discussions, we dispelled fears around trust management, showing that trusts are straightforward and supported by various resources. Let's build on this to explore the flexible nature of living trusts, which can easily adapt to life's changes. Living trusts are not rigid structures but dynamic tools that adjust as your circumstances shift. This adaptability means you can update or even revoke your trust, making it a responsive component of your estate planning. Understanding this can alleviate the fear that trusts are unchangeable, locked-in plans.

Living Trusts are Dynamic

Consider a scenario where you create a living trust as a single individual. Afterward, perhaps you will marry. In this case, you can amend the trust to include your spouse, protecting both your interests and theirs. Maybe you decide to add language that accounts for future children or stepchildren, ensuring everyone you care about is included in your estate planning. This kind of update can be done with relative ease. Or maybe there's a divorce. It's possible to modify or revoke your trust to reflect this significant life change, avoiding potential future disputes. This ensures your wishes remain current.

If children enter the picture, a living trust offers the flexibility to include provisions about guardianship or stipulate how assets should be managed or accessed while they are minors. The trust can evolve as children grow, allowing you to change distribution plans as needed. This responsiveness is a huge advantage over other forms of estate planning, which might not offer such straightforward adaptability.

The Revocation Process

What if you want to revoke your trust entirely? Doing so requires you to follow clear steps. First, determine if you have the right to revoke it under its terms. Generally, if you're the trustor, and not incapacitated, you can. You'll need to draft a revocation document, a formal piece of writing stating your intent to revoke the trust. You must sign it and have it notarized, ensuring it becomes a legally valid document. Additionally, inform all parties involved, including your beneficiaries and the trustee, about the revocation. Afterward, retitle any assets held in the trust back to your name or to another form of ownership. Proper documentation simplifies this process and prevents confusion.

Advantages of Regular Updates

Regular updates to a trust are advisable. They ensure your plan aligns with current laws and prevents disputes among heirs. With inevitable changes in tax laws and legal reforms, staying updated maximizes your trust's effectiveness. Remember to communicate these updates to beneficiaries, keeping everyone informed about their roles or potential changes to the trust's terms. Transparency helps prevent misunderstandings and conflicts later on.

Common Pitfalls to Avoid

People often fall into pitfalls when managing trusts, such as failing to properly document changes or not communicating with beneficiaries. These missteps can lead to complications, such as legal battles over trust terms or questions about your intentions. To avoid these issues, documenting every change is vital. This means creating and maintaining a clear paper trail of all amendments, revocations, and communications related to your trust. Ensuring that all involved parties have access to the necessary information prevents future legal challenges. Beneficiary communication is also essential. Keep them informed about their roles or any changes to the trust to ensure a mutual understanding of your plans and expectations.

Consider the example of a business owner who includes their business in a trust. As the business grows or changes, trust terms can be altered to reflect new business partners, changes in structure, or shifts in business interests. This aligns the trust with the evolving business landscape, maintaining relevancy. Through regular trust reviews, the business owner can adapt to new laws or ownership changes without substantial legal complications. Acknowledging this adaptability highlights that living trusts are not a "set-it-and-forget-it" solution but an evolving strategy that works best when actively managed.

Inherent flexibility makes living trusts ideal for accommodating life's unpredictability. Their design ensures they cater to personal needs and reflect your changing priorities and goals. This changes the perception of trusts as inflexible into a dynamic tool that evolves with your life circumstances. Many misconceptions stem from misunderstanding this adaptability, so it's important to refocus on how trustworthy and flexible these trusts can be.

Ultimately, the living trust stands as a testament to personalized estate management. It aligns perfectly with your objectives, provided you actively manage it. Recognizing the importance of flexibility and adaptability in living trusts shifts perspectives, encouraging their broader adoption. As you navigate life's changes, a new marriage, a growing family, a career shift, an adaptable trust can accommodate these changes, ensuring your estate plan remains relevant and beneficial for all involved.

Conclusion

Now that we've busted some of the myths surrounding living trusts, it's clear how accessible and essential they can be for everyone, not just the wealthy. Whether you are deciding how to pass down heirlooms or a small savings account, a living trust simplifies these choices without overwhelming legal costs. With this insight, we're set to explore even more about making strategic estate decisions, such as navigating tax implications in future discussions, all while keeping peace of mind front and center.

In the next chapter, we'll explore how to navigate sensitive estate planning conversations, ensuring open communication and trust among family members.

Chapter 9: Communication with Family

Have you ever found yourself wondering how to talk about sensitive topics with your family, especially something as complex as estate planning? Maybe you've thought about it but quickly brushed it aside, fearing that the conversation might lead to misunderstandings or even disputes. It's not uncommon. Many families struggle with this. You might ask yourself, "How do I bring up such a topic without causing tension?" or "What if my family doesn't agree on how things should be handled?" These are real concerns that many face when thinking about discussing their future plans.

In this chapter, we'll explore strategies to help guide these important conversations with your family. Whether you're trying to figure out the best way to start these discussions or looking for ways to ensure everyone feels heard, you'll find practical advice here. We'll focus on encouraging open communication and building trust within your family to ensure estate planning discussions are handled with honesty and respect.

Importance of Open Communication

Engaging in meaningful conversations about estate planning isn't just about the paperwork. You need to build trust within your family through open communication. The power of dialogue in family dynamics is profound. When you embrace transparency, you lay down a foundation where every member feels understood and respected. This invites an atmosphere where fears and concerns can be voiced without apprehension of judgment. It's this very openness that prevents misunderstandings from snowballing into conflicts later on. Take, for example, the case of a family that held a series of candid talks about their future plans. Open discussions about preferences led to the discovery of common values and aligned expectations. It became easier to reach a consensus on asset distribution, which brought clarity and unity.

Clarifying Intentions and Expectations

Within families, clear declarations about estate planning serve as preventive measures against potential disputes. When a parent openly communicates their intentions regarding property shares to their children, it fosters a sense of fairness and reduces misunderstandings. Transparency strengthens relationships and creates a sense of empowerment. When every family member understands their role in the planning process, it promotes collective ownership. This encourages collaboration, as each person feels their input is valued. The process becomes a shared effort rather than a source of conflict.

Look at scenarios where withholding information has strained relationships. A particular instance involved a family that avoided discussions altogether, thinking it would avert conflict. Instead, when unspoken plans came to light unexpectedly, disappointment took root. Embracing open communication earlier could have kept misunderstandings at bay, mitigating emotional fallout. Discussing such weighty topics ahead of time equips families to confront problems together, supported by mutual trust rather than animosity.

Modeling Healthy Discussion Skills

A variety of methods can ease the tension around estate planning. Many find it helpful to start conversations with personal anecdotes. Storytelling allows members to connect through shared histories, helping to build empathy and understanding. Sharing personal stories can ease tension and pave the way for honest and meaningful conversations. In one example, a mother shared her struggles with her parents' estate planning. This led her children to appreciate the complexity of the process and motivated them to articulate their own wishes clearly. It underscored how transparency today could spare them similar struggles tomorrow.

Timely Conversations

Choosing the right time and place is important, too. Just as important topics can't flourish in fleeting moments, these conversations need dedicated space and reflection. Families who allocate uninterrupted time often find that discussions are more productive and less anxiety-inducing. It's worth noting the positive framing of conversations. When approached with a focus on mutual benefits and future security, rather than obligations and fears, estate planning becomes celebratory of shared goals rather than a burden.

Imagine the comfort in knowing that everyone has been heard. It's common for people to assume their perspectives are understood based on the length of the relationship alone, especially in families. However, assumptions are slippery foundations. Encouraging genuine dialogue ensures all sides are acknowledged. Take families who engage in regular discussions, for instance. They've reaped the benefits of having fewer surprises because there's ongoing clarity about responsibilities. The consistent exchange of ideas creates bonds that withstand the test of time's pressures and uncertainties.

No conversation is perfect, but the attempt itself is a step toward understanding. A culture of openness, cultivated over time, leads to stronger, cohesive relationships. Encouraging open dialogue about estate planning helps foster meaningful connections and strengthens family communication for the future. The outcome is a cohesive family, linked by intentions that align with cherished values and mutual respect. Open dialogue on estate planning focuses on managing assets while also recognizing each member's voice and presence, strengthening family bonds beyond financial matters.

As families acknowledge each other's opinions and intentions, the next logical step involves practical strategies for starting these discussions. Looking ahead to the upcoming section, establishing the right environment is essential. Selecting environments that foster tranquility encourages families to engage in open, meaningful discussions. Sharing personal stories also establishes a strong bond among family members. It's about turning the abstract into tangible experiences, weaving warmth into what might feel like a cold, logistical undertaking.

It's essential to maintain a positive frame. When discussions emphasize benefits, like securing a comfortable future for loved ones, they inspire a shared vision. An open dialogue can then flourish, much like a garden tended by all hands. Everyone gets a chance to plant their thoughts, to nurture the ideas that will thrive into familial harmony. Bridging into the next section is about preparing the fertile ground for these strategies, allowing them to blossom within the prior discussion's context.

How to Initiate Conversations

When family members engage in transparent dialogue, it builds trust and fosters an environment where everyone feels included and valued. Trust, in turn, leads to active participation, which is required to ensure that estate planning discussions are productive and constructive. In this section, we explore practical strategies to help you begin these important conversations with your family in a way that feels comfortable and constructive.

Choosing the Right Time and Place

One of the most critical elements in starting discussions about estate planning is choosing the right time and place. Timing and location can significantly influence the mood and receptiveness of family members. Calm and neutral settings, such as a quiet living room or a favorite family spot, can help ease anxiety. These environments create a space where everyone feels more open to share and listen. Consider family gatherings as natural opportunities for these dialogues. Such settings often remind everyone of their shared bonds and can thus reduce tension around sensitive topics.

Scheduling specific times for these discussions further underscores their importance. It signals to family members that estate planning is a priority and that it deserves dedicated attention and thought. Setting a date and time gives everyone an opportunity to prepare mentally, reflect on concerns, and bring valuable input to the table. It turns a potentially casual chat into a structured and meaningful conversation.

Starting with Personal Experiences

Integrating personal experiences into these discussions can make the topic of estate planning less intimidating. Sharing a personal story about why you decided to begin estate planning can humanize the subject for others. Maybe you had a friend who went through a difficult time as a result of poor estate planning, and this motivated you to take proactive steps. Opening up about your reasons encourages others to share their thoughts and feelings, which makes the conversation more relatable and engaging.

Additionally, storytelling can soften the perception of estate planning as merely legal and financial maneuvering by highlighting its emotional significance. This allows family members to see the value in discussing such plans as a means of protecting and securing the family's future. Frame the conversation positively to emphasize collaboration rather than potential conflict. Present estate planning as an opportunity to come together to ensure that everyone's wishes are respected, which helps create a shared goal for the family.

Framing the Conversation Positively

It's also essential to highlight the benefits of organized planning. Reassure your family that these discussions aim to establish clarity and prevent potential distress in the future. Focusing on how organized planning can avert misunderstandings and unnecessary disputes shifts the conversation toward achieving constructive goals.

Promoting an atmosphere where questions and dialogue are encouraged can further foster collaboration. Welcoming questions early can help clarify misunderstandings and ensure all voices are heard. For example, when a family member asks how a specific asset will be divided, it provides an opportunity to explain and discuss various viewpoints and potentially reach consensus. This openness shows that every perspective matters, and the discussion is not just top-down but rather a collaborative effort.

Approaching discussions with an open mind is critical. An open-minded attitude makes family members feel it's safe to express their concerns without fear of judgment or dismissal. They know their input will be seriously considered, which can alleviate fears and build trust within the group. This dynamic involves active listening, where everyone attentively hears and respects each other's opinions and solutions.

Estate planning conversations can be challenging, but these strategies can create a positive and inclusive environment. They encourage participation and engagement, making discussions more productive. As you implement these approaches with your family, remember that the objective is to maintain harmony and ensure everyone's voice is heard.

The next section will help in tackling any conflicts that might arise during these discussions. While starting conversations constructively is vital, maintaining respect and harmony can sometimes be a challenge. We will discuss techniques for navigating potential family conflicts, building on the cooperative foundations established here.

Avoiding Family Conflicts

Establishing Ground Rules

Setting ground rules is one of those tasks that can seem a bit difficult at first, but they can truly revolutionize the way families communicate, especially when talking about estate planning. These rules don't have to be complex. Think of them as a collective agreement to foster respect and understanding: guidelines that encourage active listening, where each family member gets an uninterrupted say, and speaking only when someone has finished. Setting these basics helps keep conversations focused and significantly reduces the chances of heated emotions steering the discussion off course. As partners in this process, everyone knows they'll get their chance to speak, making it less likely that rivalry takes over.

Family discussions about future planning often touch on sensitive subjects, stirring emotions ranging from nostalgia to uncertainty. By having discussions with common goals, the family can shift its attention from personal wants to improving together. For example, when a family collectively agrees to preserve the ancestral home, this shared goal transforms potential competition into collaboration, fostering better dialogue and more effective decision-making. Each family member's viewpoint holds value, and the diversity of perspectives becomes a strength. Ensuring everyone feels their contributions matter promotes greater cooperation and leads to more productive outcomes.

Emphasizing Mutual Goals

But what happens when conflict arises? Nobody enjoys conflict, but addressing disagreements early is an invaluable strategy. When ignored, small misunderstandings can fester into large disagreements, complicating estate planning efforts. Tackling issues head-on allows families to learn more about each other's viewpoints and devise routes through conflicts. Consider when siblings disagree on asset distribution. Opening up about these disagreements allows room for negotiation, understanding the motives behind each viewpoint, and often reveals gaps in the family's current plan that can be closed for a more inclusive outcome.

Choosing a Mediator

Sometimes resolving these conflicts requires an unbiased ear. Mediators offer precisely this. Acting as facilitators, they can guide difficult conversations back to productive pathways. There was a case with a family where, despite several meetings, they couldn't align on how to handle future living arrangements for the eldest generation. The mediator helped set a roadmap where everyone's concerns were validated. As each person's perspective gradually unfolded, the family crafted a plan that balanced different needs, demonstrating how an external viewpoint can provide valuable clarity in sensitive discussions.

In every approach, whether setting ground rules or engaging external support, the underlying idea remains the same: fostering an environment of respect where differing opinions are allowed to be honed into collaborative decisions. It's a practice of turning potential discord into harmony, ensuring that family dynamics strengthen rather than weaken estate planning efforts.

When discussing personal and shared legacies, try to view disagreements as chances to understand each other better rather than as obstacles. Every conversation is an opportunity to strengthen family connections and improve future planning together. Protective measures, like consulting with mediators and setting collective goals, support smoother discussions, and encourage a shared vision. Recognizing that estate planning is not a one-time conversation, but an ongoing dialogue can aid in easing tensions and nurturing a landscape where each family member feels heard and appreciated.

Families create a cooperative atmosphere by taking these steps, where conflicts are seen not as barriers, but as bridges that enhance collective understanding. It assures that when it comes time to turn discussions into decisions, the groundwork laid fosters smoother transitions and enduring family relationships. This approach reinforces the practicalities of estate planning and the empathy and understanding vital to keeping a family strong and united over generations. Remember, the goal isn't just about the assets but about the people and the values they hold dear.

In all of this, remember that conversations about estate planning require time, space, and a fair environment to flourish. Creating an environment that fosters open communication, embraces diverse opinions, and uses conflict as a learning opportunity allows families to navigate estate discussions more effectively and avoid common pitfalls. With practice, patience, and a few well-placed ground rules, your family's journey through estate planning can indeed be a collaborative, empowering exercise.

Sharing Estate Planning Documents with Family

In the previous discussion on avoiding family conflicts, we focused on setting mutual goals and ground rules. These techniques build an essential groundwork for trust and openness. Now, we shift to how sharing estate planning documents with family can enrich this environment. Sharing these documents is the next logical step in promoting transparency and fostering cooperative family dynamics.

When families lack information, misunderstandings, and misinterpretations can cause unnecessary tension. Sharing estate planning documents helps everyone involved understand the decisions made and the reasoning behind them more clearly. Take, for instance, a family unsure about the division of an estate. Without access to the will or trust documents, they might make assumptions that could lead to disputes. Giving them access to these documents, however, provides clarity and averts potential conflicts.

Building Trust Through Transparency

Estate planning can be a sensitive topic, often leading to concerns about fairness and intent. Transparency in decision-making helps alleviate doubts and strengthens trust among family members. When estate planning documents are openly shared, it eliminates misinterpretations about intentions and allows loved ones to better understand each other's perspectives.

For instance, a parent who explains their decision to divide assets in a particular way can prevent feelings of resentment or confusion later. Openly sharing documents reassures family members that decisions were made thoughtfully, taking into account legal and financial considerations. This clarity fosters peace of mind, ensuring that each person understands the rationale behind key choices.

Furthermore, trust is strengthened when family members are informed about one another's wishes. Knowing the details of an estate plan, including inheritance, responsibilities, or healthcare directives, creates a sense of security. Instead of relying on assumptions, family members can approach estate planning as a collective effort aimed at securing their shared future.

Providing Clarity on Roles and Responsibilities

Estate planning involves assigning roles such as executors, trustees, or beneficiaries. These roles carry significant responsibilities, yet confusion often arises when family members are unaware of their duties. Sharing estate planning documents ensures that everyone involved understands their specific obligations, reducing uncertainty.

For example, the designated executor of an estate needs a clear understanding of their role in managing assets, paying debts, and carrying out the deceased's wishes. If this information is withheld until after the estate owner passes away, the executor may face unnecessary stress and complications. Instead, early disclosure of roles allows individuals to seek legal guidance or familiarize themselves with procedures.

Moreover, defining responsibilities helps those involved carry out their duties with confidence. A sibling assigned as a healthcare proxy, for instance, will feel more prepared to make medical decisions if they are aware of the instructions in advance. Sharing estate planning information early avoids unexpected surprises and ensures smoother transitions in the future.

Enabling Informed Discussions

Family conversations surrounding estate planning tend to be more constructive when all members have access to the same information. Having clarity on what the estate plan entails allows loved ones to focus on logistics rather than speculation. It also enables open discussions about concerns, emotions, and values tied to estate decisions.

For example, a family may wish to keep an ancestral property rather than selling it. If estate planning documents explicitly outline how the property will be managed, family members can discuss practical strategies for upkeep or financial contributions. Without such transparency, disagreements over the property's future could arise, potentially causing tension.

Knowing the specifics of an estate plan also allows you to express concerns in a timely and respectful manner. If a parent plans to allocate more inheritance to one child due to special needs, discussing this intention beforehand prevents misunderstandings. Families can work together to explore solutions that ensure fairness while respecting the unique circumstances of each member.

In addition to financial matters, estate planning discussions provide an opportunity to address deeper considerations, such as values and legacy. Conversations about what an estate represents, whether as a financial safety net, an opportunity to support charitable causes, or a means of passing on cultural heritage, help align family expectations and intentions.

Encouraging Document Updates

Estate planning requires periodic reviews to ensure documents reflect current family dynamics and legal regulations. Sharing estate planning documents encourages regular updates by inviting discussions about changes and evolving needs.

For instance, if a family welcomes a new member through marriage or birth, updating beneficiaries may become necessary. Keeping family members informed about such revisions ensures that estate plans remain accurate and representative of existing relationships. In contrast, failing to communicate updates can result in outdated legal documents that do not account for important life events.

Moreover, involving loved ones in conversations about estate planning updates fosters a sense of engagement and expression. When family members feel included, they are more likely to approach the topic with openness rather than hesitation. This practice also reinforces transparency, ensuring that all parties remain aware of significant modifications rather than being caught off guard during critical moments.

Regular updates provide an opportunity to address shifting financial landscapes or health concerns. For example, a grandparent who previously appointed one child as a trustee may later decide to divide responsibilities among multiple children to ease the workload. Discussing such adjustments ensures that those affected understand the reasons behind the change and are prepared to fulfill their roles effectively.

Sharing estate planning documents with family members is a key step in promoting transparency, reducing misunderstandings, and strengthening relationships. Fostering trust through open disclosure, clarifying roles and responsibilities, enabling informed discussions, and encouraging periodic updates transforms estate planning into a collaborative process rather than a source of uncertainty.

Families who approach estate planning with openness and honesty can ensure that future transitions occur smoothly. Transparent communication helps loved ones understand intentions, prevents conflicts, and instills confidence in the decision-making process. In essence, estate planning is about securing harmony, protecting relationships, and honoring the legacy of those who plan ahead.

Conclusion

Understanding the importance of open communication in estate planning helps families build trust and avoid misunderstandings that often lead to conflict. When everyone is heard and valued, decisions about asset distribution become easier and more transparent, fostering a sense of fairness and unity. As you move forward with your own estate planning, remember that through open dialogue, you can create a lasting legacy of trust and understanding within your family. Encouraging these conversations now ensures smoother transitions in the future, protecting both relationships and assets. With this foundation, you're well-prepared to understand the practical strategies for initiating and maintaining meaningful discussions with your loved ones, turning what might seem daunting into an empowering and collaborative experience.

In the next chapter, we'll explore the importance of updating and revoking living trusts, ensuring your estate plan stays aligned with life's changes.

Chapter 10: Updating and Revoking Living Trusts

Imagine sitting down at a family gathering, excited to share your plans for your estate with your loved ones. You've always been confident in the decisions you made when setting up your living trust years ago. But as everyone settles into conversation, you start to wonder if those plans still reflect your current wishes. Your daughter shares stories of her new business venture, while your son talks about his growing family. Suddenly, it hits you that life has changed so much since you first created that trust. And with those changes come the realization that maybe your trust, just like your evolving family dynamics, needs a fresh look.

This chapter discusses why updating and even revoking living trusts isn't just an administrative task but a necessary step in keeping your estate plan relevant and aligned with life's unpredictable journey. From significant life events to changing asset ownership, we'll explore how these factors can prompt essential updates to ensure that your intentions are clearly reflected, securing peace of mind for both you and your heirs.

Circumstances Requiring Trust Updates

Recognizing when it's time to update a living trust is important in managing your estate effectively. Life doesn't stand still, and neither should your estate plan. Think of a living trust as a blueprint. It guides the distribution of your assets, but like any plan, it needs to be revisited to reflect your current wishes and circumstances. One might draft a trust with the best intentions, yet without regular updates, even the most well-thought-out plan can become obsolete.

Major Life Events

Consider significant life events like marriage or divorce. They're pivotal moments that often require a reassessment of your estate planning priorities. Let's imagine you've recently gotten married. Without updating your trust, your new spouse might not have the legal protection or access to assets you intend for them. This could lead to a host of issues, especially if something were to happen unexpectedly. Similarly, a divorce can dramatically shift your intentions. Perhaps your former spouse was a primary beneficiary, but failing to update your trust could mean they inadvertently remain so. This oversight could lead to unintended distribution, potentially leaving loved ones and new partners unprotected.

Births and adoptions also change the dynamics in significant ways. Expanding your family usually means you wish to include new members in your estate planning. Failing to update your trust to include a new child or grandchild could result in them being disinherited, not due to intention, but due to oversight. This is particularly important if specific assets or responsibilities were meant for them. Imagine having set aside a sum of money in trust for a child's education, yet because they weren't officially added to the trust, those funds might not reach them.

Changes in Asset Ownership

Changes in asset ownership also necessitate updates to your living trust. Acquiring significant assets such as real estate, businesses, or substantial financial investments needs to be reflected in the trust. For instance, purchasing a new property that isn't included in your trust could result in that asset going through probate, defeating a key purpose of the trust. On the flip side, selling an asset might shift how your estate is divided among beneficiaries. If you don't adjust the trust to account for these changes, it could lead to confusion or disputes among heirs.

Changes in Law

Another factor prompting updates is the evolution of laws and regulations surrounding trusts and estates. Legal revisions might open up new possibilities for asset protection or tax deductions. Staying aligned with current laws can optimize a trust's benefits for inheritance and tax purposes, while neglecting such changes can lead to compliance issues, triggering potential penalties.

Updating requires clear instructions and guidance, which helps maintain the trust's integrity. Let's say there's a directive in your trust that distributes a specific asset to a charity, yet you've shifted your philanthropic focus elsewhere. Not revising this could mean another organization misses the support you originally intended.

Updates are not just about adjusting to new realities but also about preemptively safeguarding against future challenges. They ensure the seamless transition of assets, maintaining the alignment of your estate plan with your overarching intentions. This ongoing diligence reduces the likelihood of misunderstandings or disputes, providing peace of mind that your legacy is both protected and respected.

Consequences of not Updating

Let's understand the consequences of not updating a trust. Failing to revise could either mean assets are distributed in ways that no longer align with your wishes, or it could lead to crucial assets not being protected as intended. This lack of alignment becomes particularly troublesome in complex family dynamics, like those involving stepchildren or blended families. Without precise updates specifying who receives what, the risk of legal challenges increases, leaving the estate vulnerable to litigation.

Moreover, tax implications can arise from unmanaged changes in assets. Acquisitions or liquidations can shift your tax positions, affecting how burdens are shared among beneficiaries. An updated trust can mitigate potential tax liabilities, ensuring that the distribution process remains equitable and efficient. Regularly revisiting the trust allows you to take advantage of tax benefits, such as estate tax allowances, which help preserve more of your estate for your beneficiaries.

Thinking through these scenarios can help you view updating your trust not as a difficult task, but as a valuable opportunity. It's a chance to engage with your legacy actively, ensuring that it evolves alongside your life. Consider regular reviews of your trust an integral part of personal and financial management. Some individuals establish a routine of revisiting their trust annually or following any substantial change in circumstance. This proactive approach allows for the accommodation of both anticipated changes and unforeseen shifts.

The upcoming section will continue by providing clear, actionable steps to facilitate these updates. It will guide you through reviewing your trust documents, drafting necessary amendments, obtaining the required signatures, and effectively communicating modifications to all involved parties. Taking these steps ensures your estate plan remains as dynamic and unique as the life you lead, continuously reflecting your current intentions and circumstances.

How to Update a Living Trust?

Reviewing Current Trust Documents

The primary step to updating a living trust is reviewing your current documents. This step is non-negotiable. You have to know what you're working with before you tweak anything. For instance, if you've recently gotten married, you need to verify the existing terms, such as who your beneficiaries are and how assets are distributed. Sometimes, divorce means someone needs removing, or new beneficiaries added. It's like going through your wardrobe before deciding what to keep, toss, or alter. Once you understand your trust's current state, you can make informed updates.

Drafting the Amendments

Drafting amendments is where things get hands-on. You want to compile every change comprehensively, and clarity is imperative here. It might sound over difficult, but it's simply a matter of laying out the changes in plain, straightforward language. An example:

when adding a new beneficiary to accommodate a new family member, be explicit about what's being allocated to them. Avoid any legalese that might create confusion; simplicity wins every time. Think of it as providing instructions to someone using your umbrella of assets, making sure they know what they're getting into without doubting what you mean

.

Obtaining Necessary Signatures

Moving along, obtaining necessary signatures cannot be overstated. Legally, all trustees and beneficiaries need to sign off on any amended sections for these changes to hold water. It's about solidifying trust and integrity. There's an implicit contract between you and your beneficiaries, and signatures are that contract's ink. This simple act can prevent future disputes that might arise from misunderstandings about who gets what.

Communicating Changes

Communicating changes is a step that's easy to overlook but essential for transparency. It's more than just notifying people of updates. You have to foster understanding and peace of mind among everyone involved. Consider it from a family member's perspective. Knowing the changes acknowledges their involvement and assures them there are no surprises down the road. Sharing updates nurtures open lines of communication, ensuring that family dynamics stay positive. Everyone knowing where they stand avoids resentment, and fosters a cooperative environment moving forward.

The final aspect we need to touch upon is the trust's flexibility, which gets us ready for the next important topic—revoking a living trust. Living trusts offer leeway that can adapt to life's twists and turns. Understanding how to revoke a trust will expand your knowledge of managing your estate with ease and foresight. It's not just about ending a trust but knowing the methods available for revocation and how assets should be handled afterward.

There's a wealth of freedom embedded in how you manage your estate, ensuring your intentions remain achievable no matter what changes life throws at you. Let's dive into the mechanisms of revocation and what it entails in the upcoming section. You'll find that by navigating these waters skillfully, you can maintain the flexibility and relevance of your trust to fit any stage of your life.

The Revocation Process

A living trust provides flexibility in estate planning by allowing you to manage your assets during your lifetime and designate how they will be distributed upon death. However, life circumstances may change, requiring the modification or complete revocation of a trust. Understanding the revocation process is crucial for making informed decisions and ensuring that the dissolution of a trust is handled efficiently and legally.

Understanding Revocation

Revocation refers to the formal act of nullifying a living trust, effectively dissolving all legal and financial responsibilities associated with it. This step should be approached with careful consideration, as it can have significant repercussions on asset distribution, estate management, and family dynamics.

When a trust is revoked, all assets originally placed within it must be reassigned or transferred to new ownership structures. If not managed properly, the revocation may create uncertainty regarding property rights, taxation, and beneficiary interests. Before moving forward, you should evaluate your financial goals and determine whether revocation aligns with your current intentions.

A clear understanding of the revocation process empowers you to proceed with confidence, reducing the risk of confusion or unintended consequences. It is essential to recognize that revocation eliminates the protections and benefits initially established by the trust, such as avoiding probate or ensuring a structured inheritance plan. Proper documentation and careful planning can help facilitate a smooth transition while preserving your estate's integrity.

Methods of Revocation

There are multiple ways to revoke a living trust, and the method chosen should align with legal requirements and personal circumstances.

The most legally sound method of revoking a trust is through a formal written revocation document. This document explicitly states the intent to dissolve the trust and must be signed by the grantor. Some states may require notarization or witness signatures to ensure the document holds legal weight.

Drafting a formal revocation document mitigates misunderstandings among beneficiaries and other interested parties. It eliminates ambiguity and provides a clear legal record of the decision to dissolve the trust.

Revocation often affects multiple individuals, including beneficiaries and trustees. Before proceeding, discussing the decision with those involved can help minimize conflicts and ensure a smooth transition. When family members or key stakeholders understand the reasoning behind revocation, they are more likely to accept the changes and support future estate planning efforts.

While some people may express their intent to revoke a trust orally, verbal declarations hold little legal enforceability. Without documented proof, such revocations can lead to disputes among beneficiaries, causing confusion and potential legal challenges. To avoid complications, formal written documentation should always accompany revocation decisions.

Disposing of Trust Assets

Once your trust is revoked, the assets contained within it must be reassigned or redistributed. Proper handling of these assets ensures an effective transition of ownership while maintaining financial stability.

Revocation requires a structured approach to reassigning assets. Titles, deeds, financial accounts, and properties originally assigned to the trust must be transferred back to personal ownership or reassigned to another estate plan. Failing to execute transfers properly may result in ownership disputes or legal hurdles.

For example, if a home was originally transferred into a living trust, revocation requires an official deed transfer to reestablish personal ownership. Individuals should consult estate professionals or financial advisors to ensure these transfers comply with legal requirements.

Reflecting on Beneficiary Needs

Revoking a trust does not mean disregarding the financial needs of beneficiaries. It is important to communicate changes with family members or individuals who were originally designated to receive assets under the trust. Some may rely on specific distributions for financial security, and sudden revocation without explanation can cause distress.

A revised estate plan or alternative distribution method should be considered to maintain family relationships and ensure that beneficiaries are supported post-revocation.

Estate planning is an evolving process, and post-revocation asset management should reflect current financial goals. Holding ongoing discussions with family members regarding future asset allocation fosters transparency and helps prevent conflicts. Establishing a revised estate plan reassures beneficiaries and ensures a smooth transition.

Legal Considerations When Altering Trust Terms

When you think about revoking a living trust, you probably recall the meticulous steps involved. A living trust is a dynamic entity that may require adjustments over time. Imagine it's like maintaining a car. Regular maintenance ensures it runs smoothly and efficiently. Similarly, a living trust sometimes needs a tune-up based on life's changing circumstances. Both processes, revoking and modifying, require careful consideration and attention to detail. Yet, modifying a trust can be as complex as revocation, taking into account both legal and practical aspects to fully secure your intentions and interests.

State Laws Impact

Legal considerations play a central role in trust modifications. Each state has its own set of rules, and understanding these is important. For instance, if you're moving from California to Texas, you can't rely on California's laws anymore. State-specific requirements can influence everything from the language used to the witnesses needed. Ignoring these can invalidate your trust modifications. A simple error, like forgetting a notary's signature, might unravel your intentions. It's essential to research and understand these nuances or consult with an attorney who has expertise in your state's trust laws.

Potential Tax Implications

Now, let's understand the potential tax implications. Changing a trust doesn't just affect the paperwork, it might also impact your financial future. For example, if you want to add a new asset to your trust, this could alter your tax obligations. Perhaps it shifts you into a different tax bracket or affects estate taxes down the line. Understanding how modifications affect tax laws is vital. You wouldn't remodel an entire room in your house without checking how it might affect property taxes, right? The same principle applies here.

Impact on Beneficiaries

Beneficiaries form another aspect of this conversation. When modifying a trust, their interests and perspectives should be front and center. Consider a scenario where you decide to alter the percentage each beneficiary receives. Maybe you want to provide more to a child who recently had a baby or cut back on the share for someone who has become quite financially independent. These are sensitive changes that can lead to disputes if not communicated clearly. Beneficiaries have their own expectations and plans based on the current setup. Abrupt changes without discussion can strain relationships. Hence, a transparent conversation about why changes are being made can foster understanding and cooperation.

Think about real-world scenarios for a moment. You've set up a trust for your children, each receiving an equal share. Over time, one child has started a successful business, while another has pursued a career in the arts and could use more financial stability. You could modify the trust to reflect these realities. Instead of sticking to the original plan, you might decide to adjust the trust to provide more support where it's genuinely needed. This tweak can ensure the trust serves its purpose more effectively, adapting to the evolving situations of your beneficiaries.

Trust Formalities

Let's understand the formalities of these trust modifications. Documentation is key. You'd assume that merely deciding to change a trust is enough, but formal amendments must follow. Suppose you wrote an email to yourself declaring a change. While that might reflect intention, it's hardly formal enough. Legal amendments usually require precise language, must be signed, and in many cases, witnessed or notarized, depending on jurisdiction.

Compliance extends to safeguarding against unintended consequences. Let's say you're adding a new spouse as a beneficiary. If not correctly executed, this could inadvertently disinherit others. These are pitfalls where professional advice becomes invaluable. It's one thing to hold a wrench and another to know how to use it effectively without causing damage. Lawyers and financial advisers can guide you through potential risks, like accidentally triggering the need for a trust to be entirely re-evaluated or reassessed financially.

While grasping these concepts, you might feel overwhelmed, like you're learning a new language. But by breaking it down into these smaller parts, legal requirements, tax considerations, beneficiary impacts, and formalities, the pieces start to fall into place. Each element plays a role in ensuring your trust does what it's meant to do: protect and pass on your wealth and wishes.

Know that while modification is a structured process, it's also highly personal. It reflects your life's shifts—births, deaths, marriages, divorces, financial changes, and evolving priorities. Just as life situations are unique, so too are trust modifications. They are living documents, which means they should grow and evolve with you. Maintaining their relevance is in itself a form of protection, safeguarding your intentions for the future.

By now, you may see the parallels between modifying and revoking a trust. Both require an appreciation for the details, respect for legal procedures, and sensitivity toward those involved. If you're at the crossroads of considering a change, think of it as an opportunity to realign your trust with your current realities and future aspirations. A living trust should be working for you, not against you. Keeping it updated and aligned with your life's landscape preserves its effectiveness and honors its true purpose—securing peace of mind for you and your loved ones.

Conclusion

Now that we understand the essentials of updating or ending a living trust, we're better equipped to handle life's inevitable changes with confidence and ease. Think of your trust as a living document that grows alongside you. Embracing regular reviews helps protect your legacy, simplifies transitions for your loved ones, and can even save on taxes. It's like giving your estate plan a routine check-up, ensuring it stays healthy and effective. As we move forward, this knowledge empowers you to step into the future with peace of mind, knowing you're making informed choices that reflect your life's journey and aspirations. Let's be proactive about managing these details so that your estate plan continues to serve its true purpose: safeguarding your intentions and providing security for those you care about .

In the next chapter, we'll explore how to integrate digital assets into estate planning, ensuring your online presence is thoughtfully managed and protected.

Chapter 11: Including Digital Assets in Estate Planning

Many people don't consider what happens to their digital presence after they're gone. As we share photos, messages, and memories online, we accumulate a lasting digital footprint with personal and financial implications. Social media accounts store meaningful moments, while cryptocurrencies remain locked behind secure passwords. These digital assets represent personal experiences and untold stories that contribute to a person's identity.

As we increasingly integrate digital activities into our lives, from banking to building online communities, these assets demand thoughtful planning for their future. This chapter explores how to incorporate your digital footprints into estate planning, ensuring they are handled according to your wishes. Whether it's securing cryptocurrency or safeguarding sentimental memories captured on Instagram, understanding how to manage these assets can prevent confusion for those you leave behind and protect your legacy in the digital age.

Understanding Digital Assets

In today's increasingly digital world, digital assets have emerged as a significant component in the landscape of estate planning. So what exactly are we dealing with when we talk about digital assets? Essentially, a digital asset is anything you own or control that exists in a digital format. Think of things like your social media accounts, email accounts, and the data stored in them. Add to that the photos, videos, and documents you store in the cloud. Then there are cryptocurrencies such as Bitcoin or Ethereum, which are entirely digital forms of currency. Even frequent flyer miles, online subscriptions, blogs, and online storefronts fall under the digital asset umbrella.

They contribute to your digital footprint, playing a big role in defining your estate. Most people are surprised to realize that the tweets you post, the cryptocurrencies you trade, and the digital music collections you've painstakingly curated have value, some intrinsic, some financial, and some sentimental. As part of one's estate, these digital assets need careful consideration during estate planning. When treated like traditional assets, they can prevent family disputes, ensure a smooth transition of ownership, and protect your digital legacy.

Understanding your digital estate begins by taking stock of what you actually own or control digitally. Give a thought to how these assets may play out in real scenarios. Remember that encrypted drives or accounts locked behind passwords can be inaccessible to your beneficiaries unless you make specific provisions. Can't help but visualize leaving behind an Instagram account that turns into a memorial page or a blog that keeps generating income after you're gone? Each of these situations highlights the importance of identifying and including digital assets in estate planning. Knowing what assets you have empowers you to guide their inclusion in living trusts, similar to how you would with physical assets like property or bank accounts.

The Rise of Digital Assets

The value of digital assets is continuously growing in our modern estates. Cryptocurrencies have surged in popularity and often carry substantial financial worth. E-commerce businesses can continue to generate significant revenue, and often, your digital presence has an ongoing personal or cultural value. As digital assets become more significant, it's important to integrate them seriously into your estate plan. This encourages an active approach, prompting you to include your digital possessions along with tangible assets. Look at this from the financial, sentimental, and influence perspective, and it's clear why action is needed. Recent trends show increasing dependence on digital solutions for things traditionally done in analog form, shaping our future planning needs.

Legal Recognition of Digital Assets

Legally, the concept of digital assets is still catching up with traditional asset handling. This can pose challenges, especially when it comes to accessing digital assets post-death, since not all states have comprehensive laws in place. Many platforms have terms of service agreements that limit access to accounts to ensure user privacy, which means that relatives or attorneys might not automatically gain access. This reality underscores the necessity of creating clear instructions and permissions. By appointing digital executors—a trusted person empowered to manage your digital affairs—you safeguard against potential conflicts.

Concrete steps in this area involve proper documentation. Much like having a physical key for a safety deposit box, maintaining a list of passwords and account information in a secure location can prevent major headaches. Designating a digital executor who understands not just the technological aspect but also respects your wished legacy smooths this somewhat rocky terrain. Plus, this straightforward step circumvents any legal ambiguities, ensuring your digital estate is handled according to your intent.

There are practical examples of these concepts at play all around us. Consider prolific online writers who arrange to have their unpublished work handled posthumously, or social media influencers who prepare their digital legacies long before stilling their presence. Their groundwork can prevent the ambiguity that often leads to disputes among heirs who may have their own interpretations. Without the foresight of proper documentation, families can become embroiled in legal battles simply because they don't know or can't access what exists in the digital domain.

As we transition to understanding more deeply how to manage these digital assets effectively, beginning with their inventory is essential. Documenting all your digital holdings, organizing related security information, and ensuring frequent updates safeguards its relevance over time. Regular reviews can ensure new assets added to your digital sphere aren't overlooked. Consider creating an inventory that reflects not just what you have but what it means to you and others. It's a simple yet profound process. It puts control squarely in your hands, making your digital estate almost as tangible as your physical one. This helps you get started before creating a detailed inventory, using templates, and ensuring data security—important steps in digital estate planning.

Inventory of Digital Possessions

To understand the significance of documenting digital possessions, let's take a moment to recall why defining digital assets in estate planning matters. Previously, we explored how digital assets—ranging from social media profiles to online financial accounts—form a significant part of your personal legacy. Today's world depends heavily on digital interactions, making the cataloging of these assets an increasingly significant step in estate planning. Without proper documentation, digital possessions risk being overlooked, mismanaged, or lost completely, leaving your estate incomplete.

Creating a Digital Asset Inventory

Compiling a list of digital assets is required for any comprehensive estate plan. Consider it a way of ensuring every digital aspect of your life is acknowledged and ultimately managed correctly. Even if you might feel a bit lost in the vast sea of your digital presence, breaking the process down can simplify it. Structured templates and worksheets can be instrumental here, offering a straightforward method to capture everything from blog accounts to the cryptocurrencies stored in digital wallets. These resources make legal documentation easier, allowing for accurate estate planning without requiring extensive legal expertise.

Take a digital footprint inventory like you'd take stock of physical possessions. Imagine laying out your entire life's worth of digital influence on a vast table, item by item. Identifying your digital estate begins with the tangible: emails and online banking. These connect to social media accounts, cloud storage, and e-commerce platforms. Digital purchases, such as movies, music, and books, add another dimension to your online presence. Even photos stored in digital albums count as substantial parts of your virtual existence. Documenting these assets means starting with them, listing usernames, account numbers, and pertinent details.

Equally essential is keeping track of credentials for these accounts. Passwords, security questions, and usernames hold the keys to accessing digital assets and need secure and organized documentation. We suggest methods including password managers, encrypted digital storage, or even well-protected physical logbooks, which will simplify the inheritance process for the intended heirs.

Regular Inventory Updates

As you build this inventory, refreshing the information becomes vital. The digital environment is dynamic because new platforms emerge, and old ones vanish. As your usage of these platforms shifts, updates to your inventory should reflect these changes. A proactive attitude on your part ensures that estate planning keeps pace with your digital life. This means you need to regularly revise your digital asset list to prevent inaccuracies and avoid the issue of outdated digital footprints that no longer reflect reality.

Maybe you're wondering how this organization impulsively affects estate management. It's simple: clarity and transparency. A well-documented digital inventory helps heirs immediately understand the scope of what they're dealing with during the inheritance process. It shields them from potential legal challenges linked to accessing accounts they never knew existed or had forgotten.

Concrete examples offer valuable insights here. Imagine an individual who owns several cryptocurrencies. Without documenting the wallet addresses, access credentials, or backup recovery options, these assets could become permanently inaccessible. Another scenario could involve a blogger or a vlogger whose content generates passive income. Identifying these revenue streams in your digital inventory ensures ongoing benefits to heirs who may not be aware otherwise.

These illustrations showcase the importance of comprehensive documentation. However, the process must avoid redundancy, focusing on bringing fresh perspectives to each point discussed. We alleviate repetition by laying out a simple and well-structured approach and guide you effortlessly through the steps.

The journey from documenting your digital possessions to integrating them into estate planning strategies brings us to the next critical stage. With your digital landscape comprehensively mapped and logged, the logical progression is understanding how these digital assets fit into the broader picture of estate planning tools like living trusts. Here, customization becomes key, aligning with individual needs and preferences to ensure each digital asset serves its owner's desires and obligations even after they are no longer directly in command.

In wrapping up this segment, I encourage reflecting on how an organized inventory enables a seamless transition. It aids heirs in understanding what they inherit, preparing you for the next step of incorporating your digital estate into a strategic plan rather than letting it float unsupervised in the vast ether of the online world. With tools and knowledge, move forward with confidence in the security and integrity of your digital legacy, geared to be a singular component of the unique, diversified whole that is your estate planning.

Incorporating Digital Assets into Living Trusts

Just as you took time to craft a detailed digital asset inventory, you're setting the stage to decide how to incorporate these assets into a living trust. An organized inventory makes it much simpler to assess what needs protection and who should manage it. Having these digital possessions carefully listed lets you transition seamlessly into developing a plan to secure these assets for the future. The way we handle our digital footprints affects our loved ones and can either make life easier or leave behind confusion.

Choosing the Right Approach

Choosing the right approach for including digital assets in your living trust involves evaluating several strategies. You'll need to weigh your options and think about what works best for your unique situation. For instance, traditional methods such as incorporating digital assets in a comprehensive list within the trust document may offer simplicity and clarity. This approach could be beneficial for those who wish to keep things straightforward for their heirs, minimizing the steps they must take once the time comes. However, a more technology-driven strategy involves using a digital vault or secure online service specifically designed to hold access credentials and information, thereby addressing security concerns more robustly.

Consider the mix of assets you own, from social media accounts and online banking to cryptocurrency, and whether each requires different handling. Perhaps your social media presence requires basic directives for account closure or memory preservation. In contrast, your cryptocurrency might require specific instructions on accessing and managing digital wallets. In this light, blending the two strategies might serve you best, offering both the transparency of traditional methods and the security provided by digital solutions.

Including Specific Instructions

Including specific instructions in your trust documents is paramount to ensuring that digital assets are managed according to your wishes. The clearer your guidance, the less ambiguity your heirs will face, which in turn eases their administrative burden. Decide who you trust to access these assets and what level of authority they should have. For instance, granting a trusted family member the right to manage your digital library might be straightforward, but when it comes to more complex digital assets like business accounts or cryptocurrencies, you may wish to appoint someone with specialized knowledge.

Providing heirs with clear steps on how each digital asset should be managed, transferred, or even shut down ensures your intentions are honored. For example, if you have an online business, explicit instructions about who manages the continued operation or wind-down of this entity benefits everyone involved. It reduces the guesswork and keeps the process smooth, just as you intended.

Incorporating Access Information

Incorporating access information securely into your living trust is vital for empowering your heirs to fulfill your wishes responsibly. The key is balancing between whom you want to have access and maintaining security. Secure sharing of critical information might involve encrypted documents stored with your legal advisors or trusted applications designed for estate management. A practical example includes storing passwords in a digital vault like LastPass or Dashlane, which allows for safe access transfer through predetermined sharing protocols.

Addressing Account Ownership Issues

Addressing potential account ownership issues head-on will further prevent future legal tangles. Digital assets can present unique challenges not seen with traditional ones due to varied terms of service agreements or platform-specific conditions. You must thoroughly understand ownership rights to bypass these hurdles effectively. Imagine you hold a substantial amount of cryptocurrency: crypto wallets don't simply change hands easily, and differences in legislation could lead to complex situations if not addressed explicitly.

Similarly, certain online accounts, like social media, might technically belong to the service provider rather than you, affecting how they can be transferred or closed. Clearly addressing potential ownership issues in your trust documents helps ensure a smooth transition. You might specify that certain accounts be memorialized, closed, or transferred while maintaining compliance with applicable rules and regulations. Such foresight minimizes delays and preserves the estate's integrity.

As you consider all these aspects, reflect on the process of assigning digital executors. The nature of digital assets often requires individuals with particular expertise or a unique understanding of your digital world. Mention the criteria for selecting these individuals, as this will be covered in depth in the upcoming section. Knowing how to formalize their roles within your trust seamlessly ties into ensuring fluid asset management transitions.

Understanding whether your chosen executor has the necessary technical knowledge to manage assets like cryptocurrency wallets or execute complex transactions suggests who might be best suited for the role. It's important to think about how adept they are at navigating both legal responsibilities and the digital landscape.

Each of these strategic decisions aligns seamlessly with your inventory of digital assets, creating a blueprint that both protects your legacy and facilitates your heirs' responsibilities. Planning thoughtfully now makes certain that your digital possessions transition gracefully to loved ones or intended beneficiaries in the future. As we discuss about assigning digital executors next, remember that thoughtful preparation today ensures smooth transitions tomorrow.

Assigning Digital Executors

Following the previous section's exploration of the best strategies to incorporate digital assets into a living trust, the focus naturally shifts to the role of appointing digital executors. Incorporating these digital matters has become an essential part of estate planning due to the vast online presence most people maintain, often involving significant digital assets.

Definition of Digital Executors

A digital executor is someone empowered to handle your digital assets after death. Defining this role helps prevent future confusion and provides structure. Choosing the right person for this role involves more than just selecting a trusted friend or family member. It requires consideration of their technical skills and comfort with digital platforms, as well as their capacity to manage these assets in line with your wishes.

Choosing the Right Executor

To start, it's essential to have this role clearly outlined in the trust document. Explicitly state who your digital executor is and what responsibilities they hold. This clarity is vital because digital asset management often comes with unique challenges, such as navigating digital service providers' terms of service agreements. Without a well-defined authority, your digital executor might face obstacles accessing or managing your accounts.

Choose someone technically sound enough to grasp the complexities of various digital platforms, as these systems have unique protocols and legal obligations that can be difficult to navigate. For instance, some platforms strictly prohibit sharing passwords, while others might allow account transfers under certain conditions. Your digital executor should understand these nuances to avoid unintentionally violating terms that might lead to account suspension or revocation.

Educating Executors on Responsibilities

Once you've selected your digital executor, the next step is education. Equip them with a thorough understanding of their responsibilities, as well as access to necessary tools and resources to carry them out effectively. Consider setting up a meeting or a series of discussions where you explain your wishes and the specific digital assets you own. Provide documentation that outlines account numbers, usernames, passwords, and any special instructions or notes they'll need to honor your desires.

Fostering a strong relationship with your digital executor is equally important. Regular communication fosters trust and ensures alignment with your intentions. The more they understand your personal and financial priorities, the better they'll execute them after your passing. Open dialogues can help prevent misunderstandings and enhance the readiness of those who will undertake this significant responsibility.

Think of the situation where an important online business operates solely under your control. Clearly, the individual you choose as a digital executor is not only responsible for maintaining the continuity of your business operations but must also act swiftly and confidently. Without concrete directions, business operations could stall, impacting revenue and clients. Immediate access and understanding of the digital aspect of your business are pivotal. These challenges highlight why clarity and ongoing communication are essential.

Moreover, ensuring your digital executor knows how to access digital tools is vital. For example, password management tools or specific software can ease the burden of managing several digital accounts. By familiarizing them with these tools, you make the transition smoother and more efficient. This preparation also encompasses understanding digital estate laws, which can vary significantly from one jurisdiction to another. Your digital executor should be aware of these aspects, requiring some level of basic legal guidance and understanding on their part.

When discussing this role, be upfront about potential challenges they might encounter. Perhaps you have proprietary data stored in cloud services or photos, and videos meant for family that reside in private servers. Each category presents different challenges that need precise addressing. The estate planning process should involve looking into each digital asset category separately to set handling parameters.

Establishing a written and signed agreement between you and your digital executor can formalize roles and expectations. This written documentation supplements the trust and enhances clarity. It's another aspect that minimizes disputes, providing a reference point if clarity becomes an issue in execution.

The digital world is dynamic, and estate planning must keep pace to safeguard your digital legacy effectively. Ensuring clear guidance, thoughtful executor selection, ongoing updates, and robust communication sets the stage for effective management of digital and traditional assets, ultimately providing peace of mind that your wishes are honored.

Conclusion

Now that we've covered strategies for managing digital assets within a living trust, it's time to take control of your digital legacy. Understanding and organizing digital possessions, from social media accounts to cryptocurrencies, ensures seamless integration into your estate plan. Careful planning protects your digital footprint and eases the process for those you leave behind. Clear instructions and a tech-savvy digital executor are essential for maintaining your wishes. Moving forward, apply these insights to create an estate plan that balances both physical and digital assets, ensuring a smooth transition without legal complications.

In the next chapter, we'll explore accessible and budget-friendly estate planning tools, ensuring you can navigate the process confidently without unnecessary financial strain.

Chapter 12: Resource Accessibility for Estate Planning

Estate planning can feel overwhelming, with complicated legal jargon and confusing resources making the process difficult to navigate. Even setting up a basic living trust can quickly become frustrating when documents seem unclear and fees add unexpected challenges. Making important decisions for the future shouldn't feel inaccessible or overly complex, yet many people struggle to find straightforward guidance that simplifies the process.

For many, the path to effective estate planning seems filled with obstacles, both financial and informational. You're trying to secure your family's future without dipping too deeply into savings or seeking expensive legal advice. The good news is, you're not alone in this endeavor. In this chapter, we'll explore how easily accessible and budget-friendly tools, from online templates to local community resources, can transform your estate planning experience. We'll uncover these resources to empower you with the knowledge and confidence needed to take control of your financial legacy, all while keeping costs in check.

Free and Low-Cost Tools

When it comes to estate planning, the wide range of resources might feel unmanageable, but let's break it down to where it really matters—affordability and accessibility.

Online Templates

Online templates help anyone start creating living trusts. Free and low-cost options abound, crafted to cater to the myriad of state laws. You can gain a structured starting point by using these templates. This helps reduce the confusing complexity that can overwhelm newcomers. You can tailor a basic template to fit your own needs, and a little tweak here or there can morph a generic form into a personalized one. Consider how minor adaptations could help, like adding clauses that reflect your specific familial dynamics or financial interests, ultimately enhancing the template's effectiveness. You can utilize the bonus booklet provided with this book to access the necessary templates, which provide a structured starting point and help reduce errors in drafting trust documents.

DIY Trust Creation Software

Let's talk about DIY trust creation software. This tool helps you create and manage trusts on your own. This software is designed to be easy to use, much like your favorite app that feels instantly familiar. Its true strength is in its simplicity. The user-friendly interface clears away the confusion of legal jargon, making complicated concepts easy to grasp for everyone. It guides users through each stage of document creation, helping them confidently put together their own trusts. The biggest benefit? It minimizes the need for professional assistance, cutting down on costly expert consultations. It's reassuring to know that while you're supported throughout the process, you're also free from expensive advice, giving you a sense of control and independence.

Local Community Programs

Yet, sometimes, you might want the reassurance of a shared social experience. That's where local community programs come into play. Community centers and non-profits frequently step up to the plate, offering free estate planning workshops. These are important places where you can connect with others who are going through the same challenges.

Attending a community workshop can not only help you gain a clearer understanding of your next steps but also introduce you to a network of peers who become valuable allies in your estate planning journey. Such environments also allow you to tap into the expertise of volunteers and speakers who bring real-world knowledge to the table.

Public Library Resources

Local libraries serve as valuable hubs for estate planning resources, offering books, workshops, and even access to legal databases at no cost. Readers can explore insightful literature on estate planning without financial barriers, making it easier to educate themselves on the process. Additionally, some libraries host workshops led by estate planning professionals, providing practical guidance and expert knowledge. Taking advantage of these resources empowers individuals to make informed decisions, ensuring they understand their options and responsibilities without relying solely on costly professional consultations.

Bringing together, online templates, DIY software, community programs, and library resources shows that estate planning doesn't have to be too expensive. Each tool works together to create a process that is simple, affordable, and easy to use. These resources help you establish a solid plan for protecting your assets and ensuring a smooth transfer to your heirs, all while keeping costs low. Choosing this approach provides confidence, allowing you to manage your estate effectively without unnecessary financial strain.

Exploring these tools gives you direct control over your financial decisions and the legacy you want to leave. Instead of relying on expensive services and complex systems, you manage your own estate planning process. Affordable and accessible resources make it easier to make informed choices and ensure your beneficiaries are protected without unnecessary costs. This confidence supports every step of preparing a living trust that fits the demands of modern life.

Looking ahead, there is still more to discover. Each of these elements prepares you to further explore community resources and workshops that can support your estate planning efforts. These opportunities provide practical insights and encourage deeper engagement with community-led initiatives. Exploring how these resources enhance your planning process leads to a clearer understanding and a stronger sense of collaboration.

Community Resources and Workshops

In the previous section, we discussed an array of free and low-cost tools that simplify the creation and management of living trusts. These tech-driven solutions offer a remarkable leap in estate planning efficiency. However, estate planning isn't solely about leveraging technology or filling out templates. It's also about engaging with the right community resources that provide the human touch often needed for a more personalized approach to this sensitive matter.

This section focuses squarely on community resources and workshops, which play an indispensable role in the larger context of estate planning. These offerings bring enormous value by creating spaces where you can interact directly with experts. The benefit of such personal interaction cannot be overstated, as it allows for immediate feedback, shared experiences, and advice that's tailored to your unique situation. Legal professionals simplify complex terms, and connecting with them, even briefly, can instill a level of confidence that makes the whole planning process easy.

Local Bar Association Workshops

Let's start with Local Bar Association Workshops, a fantastic resource often available in most communities. These workshops stand out by providing free or low-cost informational sessions where you get face time with legal experts. Attending these sessions helps you develop a deeper understanding of the essential yet complex documents involved in estate planning. This interaction can bring much-needed clarity and reassurance. For instance, imagine attending a session where the lawyer explains the technicalities of a living trust word-by-word, enabling you to grasp concepts that once seemed complex.

Non-Profit Organizations

Another powerhouse of support is Non-Profit Organizations that focus on financial literacy, including estate planning. These groups often host webinars and workshops that cater to a wide audience, ensuring inclusivity across all financial backgrounds. They provide resources designed specifically for those who might not have excessive assets or large estates to plan for, making advice accessible to everyone. Picture a session held by a non-profit that uses simple language to break down estate taxes for middle-income families. The complexity of the topic becomes far more digestible, and families leave with a new perspective and reduced anxiety about the future.

Elder Care Resource Centers

Elder Care Resource Centers cater specifically to seniors, addressing their joint needs for immediate family planning and tackling the intersection of health and estate issues. These centers offer workshops tailored to elder-specific scenarios, like integrating medical power of attorney with financial proxies or coordinating long-term care plans with estate strategies. Let's consider an elderly couple who attend a workshop at their local resource center. Here, they learn firsthand how to efficiently merge their healthcare directives with their wills in a manner that truly reflects their wishes. This guidance empowers seniors to make informed decisions, often revealing efficiencies they hadn't previously considered.

University Programs

Universities, too, have grasped the value of contributing to community education through estate planning programs. Public events and courses create opportunities for legal students and community members to come together and work on real-world legal challenges as a team. The innovative ideas that emerge from these groups can be groundbreaking. Picture a university event where a law professor outlines emerging trends in digital assets and how they affect estate planning. Such forward-thinking education emphasizes not only learning but also engagement, fostering an environment where community members and students exchange ideas and create impactful solutions.

Real-world scenarios demonstrate how essential these community resources are. Consider Anna, a single parent in a busy urban area, feeling overwhelmed by the task of planning her estate. Without any legal background, the information online seemed too dense. She attends a monthly local bar association workshop where, after a session, she stays back to chat with a lawyer about specific concerns she has for her children's guardianship. This one-on-one interaction helps frame her thinking, provides solid next steps, and puts her mind at ease.

Or think about Javier, who, after attending a non-profit webinar on digital estate aspects, realizes he needs to account for his numerous online accounts and their value. The practical strategies shared during the webinar help him frame a comprehensive digital inventory, a step he previously wouldn't have considered. These workshops can serve as an eye-opener even for those who feel they have everything under control.

After exploring these community resources, you can seamlessly shift your attention to estate planning software options in the next section. Software provides an array of features that assist in creating and maintaining living trusts, complementing the foundation laid by the community resources you've engaged with. Such tools offer ongoing support, enabling you to apply the insights gained from human interaction in a digital environment that continually supplements your planning with updates and reminders.

By combining community support and technology, you can manage estate planning more easily. Whether you get helpful tips from a workshop or use software to stay organized, you have what you need to create a planning strategy that works for you. Remember, estate planning is as much about the relationships and human connections you forge as it is about the documents you sign and register.

Estate Planning Software

In the quest for effective estate planning, a critical aspect is accessing resources that simplify the process. Previously, we discussed community resources and workshops, which serve as foundational elements for understanding estate planning. Now, let's explore how estate planning software provides a digital extension to these learning opportunities, offering assistance beyond in-person support.

Consumer-Friendly Options

Estate planning software offers consumer-friendly features that revolutionize the whole experience. With user-friendly interfaces, these apps guide you through templates and workflows that simplify complex legal processes. Imagine facing a mountain of legal jargon and then discovering a tool that simplifies this into easy-to-follow steps. That's the power of good software. You don't need to slog through information that seems written in another language. Instead, such software provides clarity, leading to enhanced self-sufficiency.

Cost vs. Benefit Analysis

Shifting focus to the cost versus benefits of estate planning software, the financial aspect is undeniable. Hiring legal professionals can be expensive, especially if your estate requires meticulous attention. Using software solutions helps lower intimidating legal fees, offering a more cost-effective alternative. Think about the costs: hiring a lawyer could cost thousands of dollars, but spending money on software just once is much cheaper. Over time, the savings accumulate, allowing you to redirect funds to other essential financial tasks. For those with limited financial resources, this ensures estate planning remains within reach, without sacrificing quality. Essentially, it's a sound financial decision. You get robust support without the continuous worry of expenses piling up.

Accessibility on Multiple Devices

Estate planning software doesn't just sit on one computer. Its accessibility expands across multiple devices. This means managing your plans isn't constrained by location or time. Whether you're on a tablet at home, using a smartphone during a commute, or checking details on your work computer, your plans are always within reach. This flexibility is invaluable. When you need to update your living trust or modify beneficiary contact details, you won't have to schedule a formal session. The flexibility of managing these changes whenever necessary ensures convenience and efficiency in handling estate planning tasks.

Integrations with Other Financial Tools

Integration of estate planning software with other financial tools further elevates its utility. Viewing both personal finances and estate plans in a unified manner provides a holistic approach to financial management. For instance, the software might offer features that estimate potential expenses related to the tax consequences of your plans. These estimates enable you to make informed decisions about trust management.

Estate planning software bridges the gap often left by traditional methods, ensuring both efficiency and accessibility. Now, having explored these technological supports, let's peek at what lies ahead. In seeking affordable legal support without spiraling costs, one can find assistance in legal aid organizations, sliding scale services, and even online consultations. These discussions will open up pathways that allow you to access necessary support without the financial strain typically associated with legal services. Consider the next segment a continuation of empowering solutions, ensuring you remain informed and confident in every decision related to estate planning.

Finding Legal Support Without High Costs

As we transition from estate planning software, these tech tools give you the power to manage many aspects of your estate independently. Their user-friendly interfaces and integration capabilities ease the complexity involved in organizing financial documents, distributing assets, or tracking legal changes. Yet, there's a moment when digital tools aren't enough, and legal expertise becomes vital. That's where professional advice plays a significant role in ensuring your estate plan aligns perfectly with the law.

Legal Aid Organizations

Legal Aid Organizations provide an essential support network, especially if you're conscious of costs. Many regions host these groups, which offer free or significantly discounted legal services. For instance, organizations like Legal Aid Society or local pro bono clinics deliver assistance to those qualified by income. You can identify local resources by conducting a simple online search or contacting a nearby community center. Often, they cover basic estate planning needs such as drafting wills or establishing trusts, which can be incredibly reassuring if you're venturing into estate planning for the first time.

Sliding Scale Legal Services

Accessibility doesn't stop there. Another appealing option is Sliding Scale Legal Services, where attorneys adjust their fees based on your income. This model ensures fair legal representation, allowing you to afford lawyers who might otherwise be out of your budgetary reach. For instance, you've invested in estate planning software and organized your documents, but you hit a complex legal hurdle. Engaging a sliding scale attorney means tackling that challenge without breaking the bank. Perhaps you're a single parent with a modest income, or a young professional just starting out—this system recognizes your financial constraints while offering professional support tailored to your needs. It's practical, flexible, and designed to give you peace of mind.

Online Legal Consultations

Incorporating technology further, we explore Online Legal Consultations. This modern solution eliminates logistical barriers often associated with traditional consultations. Gone is the need to schedule around peak traffic times or traverse long distances for a brief meeting. With online consultations, you tap into legal advice from your living room, saving both time and travel expenses.

Post-Consultation Support

But what happens after the consultation? Many attorneys and legal professionals extend Post-Consultation Support through ongoing services at reduced rates for returning clients. After your initial meeting, you might have further questions or need additional assistance as your circumstances evolve. This practice nurtures a beneficial relationship where the legal expert becomes a continuous resource rather than a one-time consultant. For example, some practices offer follow-up appointments or document reviews at a fraction of the usual rate. This sustained support fosters a trusting relationship and ensures you feel confident and well-informed as you navigate the complexities of estate planning.

Providing accessible legal resources goes beyond affordability. The reassurance that cost shouldn't prevent you from seeking necessary legal aid is paramount. By understanding your options, such as Legal Aid Organizations, Sliding Scale Services, Online Consultations, and Post-Consultation Support, you're equipped with the knowledge to make informed decisions. Each option shows how affordable and accessible estate planning can be a reality, ensuring you protect your assets and secure your legacy, no matter your financial situation.

You can feel empowered knowing that resources at every turn ensure fair and equal access to legal support. Whether you choose to start with software, seek advice through affordable services, or continue consultations online, the pathway is clear and holistic. Tackling estate planning with this arsenal means approaching the future with confidence, knowing your plans are in place and the transitions for your heirs will happen as you intend.

Keep in mind that these tools and resources guide you, while simplifying and enhancing your ability to control your financial legacy. In essence, using available resources guarantees that estate planning becomes not just an obligation but a strategic choice aligned with your life's circumstances and goals.

Conclusion

In wrapping up our discussion on accessible and affordable estate planning tools, these resources have proven to be transformative in simplifying the process and empowering individuals to take control of their financial future. From online templates to community programs, you now have the knowledge and tools to create a plan tailored to your needs. As we move forward to the next chapter, "Community Resources and Workshops," you'll discover additional ways to enhance your understanding and engagement. With these insights, you're well-equipped to secure your financial legacy with confidence.

In the next chapter, we'll examine the real-life impact of living trusts, showing how they provide financial stability and peace of mind during life's unexpected challenges.

Chapter 13: Real-Life Applications of Living Trusts

In a quiet suburban neighborhood, the Thompsons were a picture of stability and love. With two young children and aspirations for their future, they had everything planned out—or so they thought. Life has a way of throwing challenges, even at those who plan meticulously. One morning, Mr. Thompson went for his usual jog but never returned home. The family was thrown into turmoil, not just emotionally, but financially as well. While they had thought about estate planning, like many, they hadn't fully acted on it, apart from one important step: setting up a living trust. This decision, taken after much prodding from friends, would soon transform from an abstract concept into a concrete lifeline.

As Mrs. Thompson navigated the heartbreaking days that followed, she realized the implications of their decision. Instead of stressfully managing assets through the maze of probate court, her focus could remain on helping the kids adjust to their new reality. A trusted family friend managed the finances, ensuring their children's future was secure without dipping into chaos or confusion. Throughout this chapter, we will explore stories like the Thompsons', revealing practical ways living trusts protect families, safeguard assets, and ease transitions, especially when life takes an unexpected turn.

Asset Protection for Minors

Estate planning is often associated with securing assets for heirs, but when those heirs are minors, additional safeguards are necessary to ensure financial stability. Minors lack legal capacity to manage assets independently, which can create vulnerabilities if proper estate planning measures are not in place. A living trust serves as a reliable solution, allowing parents and guardians to maintain control over financial distributions while ensuring that funds are used responsibly. This section explores how living trusts protect minors, the consequences of inadequate planning, and key considerations for parents navigating estate decisions.

Understanding Guardianship Requirements

When minors inherit assets, they cannot legally manage them until they reach adulthood. Without a structured plan, guardianship courts may step in to oversee financial matters, leading to delays and additional legal expenses. A living trust helps avoid such complications by appointing a trustee responsible for managing the child's inheritance. The trustee ensures that funds are distributed appropriately, covering essential needs such as education, healthcare, and living expenses.

Trusts also allow parents to specify when and how their child can access funds. Instead of receiving a lump sum inheritance upon reaching adulthood, minors can benefit from structured disbursements tied to milestones such as completing higher education or reaching a certain age. This prevents financial mismanagement and ensures that assets support long-term stability.

Selecting the right trustee is important. Parents often choose family members, financial advisors, or legal professionals who can act in the child's best interest. The trustee's role includes overseeing investments, managing distributions, and ensuring that assets remain protected from external claims. Defining clear responsibilities within a trust document ensures parents gain peace of mind knowing their children's inheritance is secure.

Case Example: Minor Beneficiaries

Michael and Laura, a married couple, had a seven-year-old daughter, Sophie. Concerned about ensuring her financial stability in the event of their unexpected passing, they decided to set up a living trust rather than relying on a will.

Challenges without Trust:

- If they passed away without a trust, Sophie's inheritance would have gone through probate, delaying access to funds.
- A court-appointed guardian may have controlled financial decisions instead of someone they trusted.
- If Sophie received a lump sum at 18, she might have lacked the financial experience to manage it wisely.

The Living Trust Solution:

Michael and Laura worked with an estate planner to structure a trust that outlined:

- **Staggered Distributions:**
  - Funds for education, healthcare, and living expenses could be accessed as needed.
  - A partial inheritance at age 25 for major life expenses.
  - The remaining funds at age 30, ensuring maturity before receiving full access.
- **Protection Against External Claims:** Assets were shielded from creditors or legal disputes.

Outcome and Benefits:

- Sophie's guardian had immediate access to funds for essential needs.
- The structured plan prevented financial mismanagement while providing stability.
- The family avoided probate delays and court-appointed financial oversight.

Had Michael and Laura not planned ahead, Sophie's inheritance would have been tied up in probate, potentially leaving her without financial resources when needed.

Consequences of Inadequate Planning

Failing to implement a living trust can lead to financial complications for minor heirs. Without a structured plan, courts often step in to manage inheritance matters, leading to potential delays, disputes, and unintended outcomes. In some cases, assets may be released to minors without restrictions, making them vulnerable to financial mismanagement.

Another issue arises when guardians lack clear instructions on how to distribute assets. This can lead to conflicts among family members, where different parties hold competing views on financial decisions. Without a trust document outlining specific directives, managing a child's inheritance becomes subjective rather than structured.

Additionally, minors inheriting assets without safeguards may face external risks such as creditor claims, irresponsible spending, or legal disputes over financial decisions. A trust acts as a protective barrier, ensuring assets remain secure until the child is ready to take full control of their finances.

Key Takeaways for Parents

Parents must recognize estate planning as a vital aspect of securing their children's future. Establishing a living trust ensures that financial assets remain protected, responsibly managed, and accessible when needed. This approach prevents legal complications, minimizes financial risks, and eliminates uncertainties surrounding asset distribution.

Consulting estate planning professionals is beneficial when structuring trusts. Legal advisors can help define trust provisions, designate responsible trustees, and establish flexible terms that align with the child's long-term needs. Early estate planning provides peace of mind, ensuring that children inherit assets in a structured manner that promotes stability and financial security.

A well-crafted living trust ultimately serves as an investment in a child's future. Parents who take proactive steps to manage inheritance matters provide their children with financial protection while reducing the burdens associated with probate or legal disputes.

Estate planning ensures that the next generation benefits from responsible financial management and long-term stability.

Moving on to the next section, one ponders the additional benefits of living trusts, such as their power to prevent needless misunderstandings or disputes within the family. Whereas protective structures exist for assets, similarly, users can avoid tensions and familial conflicts.

Avoiding Family Disputes

In the previous section, we explored how living trusts safeguard the future of minors by providing a structured framework for asset protection. This same clarity and guidance serve another purpose: preventing misunderstandings and disputes among family members after a loved one's passing. Just as it's important to secure a child's inheritance, it's equally vital to prevent familial discord over asset distribution. A well-structured living trust provides that roadmap, ensuring every penny and piece of property goes where the deceased intended.

Conflict Avoidance through Clear Instructions

Imagine a situation where an unexpected death occurs within a family. A well-planned living trust can delineate exactly what each beneficiary receives. There's no guesswork and no room for misinterpretation. Its specific instructions grant each heir a clear understanding of their roles and expectations. This precision dramatically reduces ambiguity, which is often the root cause of disputes. For example, consider the Thompson family, who set up a living trust detailing how their assets should be divided. When Mr. Thompson passed away, the trust instructed that his eldest daughter manage and distribute funds according to outlined percentages to each sibling. Rather than descending into arguments, the siblings appreciated the clarity and fairness of the arrangement. The trust's structure reduced potential conflicts, turning a potentially traumatic family event into a testament to their father's care and foresight.

Transparency

Beyond preventing disputes, living trusts foster transparency that strengthens family bonds. Heirs understand the rationale behind them. This transparency opens dialogue among beneficiaries early, well before any emotions of grief and loss entangle the situation. It's a wise approach to conduct family meetings to discuss the trust's contents. These gatherings encourage an open environment, where everyone feels comfortable expressing concerns and ensuring any misgivings are addressed proactively. As a result, these meetings turn estate planning into a collaborative process rather than a contentious one. They help dispel the air of secrecy that sometimes surrounds financial matters, replacing it with trust and cooperation.

Legal Assurances

Legal assurances are another key advantage of living trusts that can play a pivotal role in preserving family harmony. Unlike a typical will, trusts are generally not subject to probate. This not only accelerates the process of asset distribution but also significantly reduces the chance of contestation. Adjustable terms within a trust provide robust protection against frivolous legal claims, which often arise like weeds in the aftermath of a will reading. These mechanisms ensure the deceased's wishes are enforced meticulously, reducing the likelihood of disputes and ensuring that the family's focus remains where it should be—supporting one another through grief, not engaging in protracted legal battles.

Strategies for Family Discussions on Estate Planning

Talking about estate planning can feel uncomfortable, but open communication ensures clarity and prevents future disputes. Regular family meetings create a space where everyone can express concerns, ask questions, and contribute to decisions. Keeping discussions structured and positive helps ease tensions and fosters cooperation.

To encourage participation, it's essential to create a welcoming environment where all voices are heard. Setting clear objectives for each conversation, such as discussing wills, trusts, or financial guardianship, keeps discussions productive. Inviting professional guidance, like an estate planner or mediator, can help address complex legal matters and provide reassurance.

Proactive planning prevents misunderstandings down the road. Families should approach estate discussions early rather than waiting for a crisis. Establishing expectations, documenting decisions, and revisiting plans regularly ensures that arrangements remain aligned with evolving circumstances. A well-communicated estate plan strengthens family unity and ensures a smooth transition for future generations.

As we conclude this section, the focus shifts from family arrangements to managing business interests through living trusts. Just as trusts provide a smooth transition of family wealth, they also ensure continuity in business operations, securing the future beyond individual capacity. This upcoming section will explore how living trusts can play a pivotal role for business owners, ensuring their vision continues to thrive, even after they are no longer able to guide it personally.

Managing Business Interests

Previously, we talked about how living trusts can diminish family quarrels by providing clear, legally binding instructions about asset distribution. This clarity prevents misunderstandings and disputes over personal estates. Now, let's extend that discussion to the world of business, where the stakes are often higher and the consequences of miscommunication can disrupt not only family harmony but also business operations. Just like personal estate planning, business continuity benefits from the precision and foresight that living trusts offer. The seamless transition from managing personal wealth to managing business interests underscores how living trusts are versatile tools for both realms.

Continuity of Management

This section focuses on how living trusts help manage business interests, especially during challenging times like when an owner becomes unable to make decisions or passes away. Business owners know that continuity is key. Not just maintaining operations but also staying true to the vision and ethos that have driven their success. A well-crafted living trust serves as a roadmap for successors, detailing exactly how the business should proceed, who should make decisions, and how those choices align with the owner's original goals. This clarity helps avoid disruptions and ensures the business's ethos carries on without faltering.

Continuity of management is one of the biggest hurdles a business faces when an owner becomes incapacitated or passes away. Living trusts solve this problem by naming a successor who is ready to step in. This is a thoughtful choice that reflects strategic planning. Living trusts outline management strategies, embodying the owner's philosophy and decisions, which keep the business running smoothly in line with its established customs and practices. For example, if an owner has always prioritized sustainable practices, these priorities can be enshrined in the trust so that successors maintain these values.

Case Study: Family-Owned Business

Consider a real-life example of a family-run business that used a living trust to sail through an ownership transfer without a hiccup. Imagine a small manufacturing company run by a matriarch who values quality over quantity. As she aged, she established a living trust specifying her eldest daughter as the successor, trained for years in the nuances of the family business. When she ultimately stepped down due to health issues, the transition was seamless. Her daughter took the reins without the typical legal battles or family discord many businesses face. Thanks to the trust, financial responsibilities were clear, operational priorities outlined, and the family's legacy protected. This example underscores how living trusts facilitate what can otherwise be a tumultuous time, maintaining both financial and operational stability as leadership shifts.

Involvement of Successors

Planning for the future is imperative for any successful business transition. Living trusts offer a framework for integrating successors. Training future leaders isn't about formalizing them into the business only in its later stages; it starts long before they officially take charge. Many living trusts go beyond naming a successor. They detail mentoring roles and educational pathways. These plans prepare successors by aligning them with the company's and family's long-term goals. Let's say, in our earlier example, the daughter didn't suddenly find herself at the helm by accident; she was gradually groomed for this role, balancing business school during the day with hands-on learning from her mother during evenings in the factory. The trust foresaw this structured grooming and made sure that when the baton was finally passed, she was ready in skill and spirit.

Protection Against External Claims

While living trusts ensure internal stability, they also offer protection from external threats. Businesses often stand vulnerable to outside claims, whether from creditors or legal disputes. Securing business assets within a living trust allows you to establish a legal shield that protects these assets from such claims. A living trust provides business owners with a structured defense against potential claims, ensuring that assets remain safeguarded and operational stability is maintained. Asset division within trust frameworks can prevent creditors from laying claim to family business interests, acting as a preventive measure against financial strain that might affect both the business and its stakeholders. Such preservation is crucial when the firm remains interlinked with the family's fortune and reputation.

As we bridge this discussion to what's coming next, we peer into another aspect of protection that living trusts offer. Beyond safeguarding the business, living trusts can also insulate heirs' inherited assets from creditors' prying eyes. This section will explain how living trusts protect heirs, making sure they receive their inheritance without losing it to outside claims. This protective nature of living trusts underscores their broad utility in holistic estate planning, aligning with today's narrative and adding yet another chapter in building a comprehensive safety net around family wealth and business interests.

Protecting Heirs from Creditors

Shifting from our previous discussion on managing business interests within living trusts, it's essential to understand how these same principles apply broadly, especially concerning protecting heirs from creditors. The strategies we considered earlier, continuity planning and asset protection within a trust, create a strong foundation. Now, let's explore how living trusts extend these benefits to inherited assets, providing a shield against creditor claims and ensuring seamless transitions for beneficiaries.

Estate planning ensures that heirs can access and manage their inheritance without financial setbacks. One of the biggest threats to inherited wealth comes from creditors, who may attempt to claim a portion of an heir's assets due to existing debts or legal judgments. A living trust offers a powerful solution, acting as a protective barrier that keeps inherited assets safe from external financial claims.

Understanding Creditor Claims

When heirs receive their inheritance through a will, assets typically go through probate before being distributed. During probate, creditors can make claims against an heir's inheritance, potentially reducing the amount they receive. If the heir has outstanding debts, creditors may attempt to seize assets to settle those obligations.

A living trust, however, operates differently. Because assets within a trust are not considered part of the heir's personal estate, they are shielded from creditors. Instead of assets being directly transferred to heirs, they remain under the control of the trust, ensuring long-term protection. Trust structures like spendthrift trusts provide even greater security by restricting an heir's access to funds, preventing creditors from pursuing legal claims against the assets.

Without proper estate planning, heirs may face significant financial risks, including:

- Legal battles over inheritance claims.
- Unintended asset losses due to outstanding debts.
- Disruptions to financial stability, especially if inherited assets were intended for necessities like housing or education.

Carefully structuring a living trust allows you to safeguard your family's legacy while ensuring your heirs have financial security, even in the face of creditor challenges.

Illustrative Case Example: Protecting an Inheritance

John and Lisa were a married couple who built a successful business and accumulated significant wealth. They had two adult children, Adam and Sophie. While Sophie had stable financial habits, Adam struggled with debt due to poor financial decisions and legal disputes with creditors. Concerned that Adam's inheritance could be taken by creditors, John and Lisa worked with an estate planner to protect their family's assets.

Challenges Without a Trust:

- If John and Lisa passed away without a trust, Adam's inheritance would be vulnerable to creditor claims.
- A probate court could force asset liquidation to settle outstanding debts.
- Adam's financial instability could lead to mismanagement of the inheritance.

The Living Trust Solution:

To prevent financial loss, John and Lisa established a **spendthrift trust** with the following provisions:

- **Appointment of a Trustee** – A financial advisor was selected as trustee to oversee Adam's inheritance.
- **Restricted distributions** – Adam could only access funds for essential expenses like housing and education.
- **Creditor protection** – Assets remained within the trust and were not legally considered part of Adam's estate, preventing seizure.

Outcome and Benefits:

- Adam's inheritance was protected from creditor claims, ensuring financial security.
- The structured distribution prevented mismanagement while allowing access to

necessary funds.

- Sophie, whose finances were stable, received her inheritance without complications.

Had John and Lisa not created a living trust, Adam's inheritance could have been significantly reduced or lost entirely due to legal disputes.

Strategies for Implementation

Setting up a living trust with creditor protection requires thoughtful planning. Families should take the following steps:

1. **Consult Estate Planning Professionals**
    - Working with attorneys specialized in **asset protection** ensures that trust structures align with legal safeguards.
    - Financial advisors can provide recommendations on inheritance distribution strategies.
2. **Articulate Clear Terms in the Trust Document**
    - Trust provisions should explicitly limit an heir's direct access to funds, reducing creditor claims.
    - Defining trustee roles ensures responsible asset management.
3. **Regularly Review Trust Terms**
    - Updating trust provisions based on changes in legal regulations strengthens protections.
    - Reviewing successor trustee arrangements maintains financial security for future generations.
4. **Incorporate Legal Safeguards Against External Claims**

  - Additional legal mechanisms, such as **spendthrift provisions**, reinforce asset protection.
  - Ensuring proper documentation prevents potential disputes over inheritance rights.

With these steps, families can create a secure and resilient estate plan that protects heirs from financial challenges.

Reinforcement of Legal Access

Living trusts not only secure assets but also provide heirs with a structured financial framework. Clearly defining roles within the trust enhances its enforceability, ensuring heirs receive their intended inheritance without external interference.

- Trustees oversee financial distributions, preventing reckless spending.
- Legal documents reinforce protections, reducing challenges from creditors.
- Structured inheritance planning reduces risks, ensuring assets remain intact for future generations.

Protecting heirs from creditors is a crucial aspect of estate planning. Without proper safeguards, inherited wealth may become vulnerable to external claims, leading to financial instability. A living trust offers a powerful defense, keeping assets secure while allowing heirs controlled access to their inheritance.

Families should prioritize proactive estate planning, working with professionals to structure trusts that shield assets from legal challenges. Implementing spendthrift provisions, selecting responsible trustees, and regularly reviewing estate plans ensures that heirs maintain financial security and stability while remaining protected from creditor interference.

Conclusion

In this chapter, we've seen how living trusts offer practical benefits for protecting assets and ensuring smooth transitions for heirs. Providing clear guidelines and bypassing probate allows living trusts to minimize financial burdens, offering families stability and peace of mind during difficult periods. Whether it's securing a minor's inheritance or shielding assets from creditors, these legal arrangements work wonders in simplifying what could otherwise be a complex process. As you consider your estate planning options, think about how a living trust might fit into your strategy and offer the protection and clarity your family deserves.

In the next chapter, we'll explore recent legal updates and financial strategies, ensuring estate plans remain effective and aligned with evolving regulations.

Chapter 14: Legal and Financial Trends in Estate Planning

Updating a phone ensures access to the latest security features and apps, keeping everything running smoothly. However, the same approach is rarely applied to estate plans, even though keeping them current is just as essential. Many people overlook the importance of regular updates, allowing estate plans to become outdated and ineffective. When legal and financial trends shift, an estate plan that remains unchanged may no longer provide the intended protection. Changes in laws and emerging financial practices can introduce gaps, potentially leading to complications for assets or loved ones. Ensuring an estate plan is regularly reviewed and adjusted helps maintain its effectiveness and safeguards financial security.

In this chapter, we will discuss the recent legal updates and financial strategies essential for modern estate planning. These tips will help you understand the changes and show why it's important to stay updated and ready. Whether you're looking to protect assets without breaking the bank or ensure your wishes are clear-cut, understanding these trends will empower your planning journey.

Recent Legal Updates Affecting Trusts

Living trusts have experienced significant changes across various state laws recently, and staying updated is important. These updates often influence existing trusts, which may require individuals to take preventive measures to avoid legal complications. For example, some states have modified rules regarding the duration of living trusts, which could impact the length of time assets can remain in trust. If your trust doesn't comply with the new regulations, it might need adjustment to prevent legal issues.

Additionally, some states have altered regulations concerning the default provisions for beneficiaries if a trust is deemed invalid. Understanding these changes can assist you in amending your trusts to ensure beneficiary designations align with your intentions. It protects both you and your heirs from potential legal complications or disputes, as these modifications help maintain the validity of your estate planning.

Federal Estate Tax Revisions

Federal estate tax revisions represent another important area of focus. Changes to tax regulations can dramatically influence existing estate plans, sometimes requiring reconsideration of strategies. For instance, adjustments in the estate tax exemption threshold can affect your overall tax liability. Previously, estates valued under a certain limit were exempt from taxes. However, should that threshold decrease, estates once considered exempt might now face tax obligations. Understanding these changes provides an opportunity to restructure your assets or set up new vehicles to minimize tax impacts on your heirs.

Increased tax rates or the introduction of new taxes can also significantly alter estate planning. Consulting with a tax advisor can equip you with strategies, such as gifting, to reduce the tax burden on your estate. Proper management and foresight provide peace of mind, knowing your wealth will effectively and efficiently transfer to your heirs.

Trustee Duty Regulations

Moving to trustee duty regulations, these new rules emphasize the importance of wise trustee selection. Trustees have always held significant responsibilities, but changes in regulations have increased accountability. For example, states may now demand greater transparency and reporting requirements, making it essential for trustees to be well-informed and conscientious about their duties.

Hands-on examples illustrate these duties. Trustees must now maintain detailed records of all transactions, ensuring complete transparency. They also may need to prove adherence to the best interest of the beneficiaries, fundamentally altering the selection process. Choosing someone who lacks the time or knowledge might expose you to legal consequences or asset mismanagement, highlighting the necessity of informed decision-making.

Consumer Protection Laws

Consumer protection laws play a pivotal role in estate planning as they often protect consumers from exploitation. Enhanced awareness empowers you to make informed decisions, ensuring fair practices. Laws such as providing clear disclosures on trustee fees and preventing conflicts of interest help bolster confidence and protect your wealth. Real-life scenarios, like beneficiaries protected from hefty unexpected fees due to enhanced disclosure requirements, demonstrate the impact of these protections.

These laws also ensure that financial professionals act in ways that prioritize clients' best interests. Understanding your rights under these regulations will help when you engage with service providers, such as financial advisors or estate planning attorneys. Protection from exploitative practices can mean safeguarding your assets and providing an additional security layer in your estate planning journey.

Looking ahead, consider these evolving practices as tools to further refine and advance your estate planning process. You possess the power to navigate changes effectively, safeguard wealth, and ensure future generations benefit from your planning. Stay engaged to explore further how these financial management practices integrate with new trust laws and consumer protections to create robust, lasting estate plans.

As we move forward, let's draw a connection to how these significant legal developments in estate planning seamlessly lead to evolving practices in financial management related to living trusts. The new section will guide you through investment strategies that align with your estate plans, the importance of fee transparency, and asset diversification. Investment strategies within living trusts can be complex, yet they offer opportunities for maximizing wealth. Consider exploring different asset classes or reviewing risk management practices. Fee transparency is also vital, ensuring you aren't overpaying your advisors or trustees, which protects your heirs' benefits.

Trends in Financial Management Within Trusts

Building on the recent legislative changes we discussed earlier, it's clear these shifts aren't just rulebook updates. They directly impact how you might approach financial management within your trusts. With new laws affecting estate planning, the ripple effects can mean reevaluating your financial strategies to optimize your returns and create stronger, more secure living trusts.

Investment Strategies in Trusts

One of the major changes in financial management practices within trusts is the emergence of innovative investment strategies. Consider the role of sustainable investing. Not too long ago, it was a niche consideration, but now, more investors are aware of how environmental, social, and governance (ESG) factors influence financial performance. Including ESG-compliant options in your trust portfolio could potentially increase returns while aligning your investments with personal values. Additionally, the integration of alternative investments, such as private equity or real estate, could provide balance and stability, particularly in unpredictable markets. The key is to explore diverse asset management that covers various types of investments to enhance the overall performance of your trust.

Fee Transparency Developments

Another shift worth noting is the trend towards fee transparency. This trend reflects a broader push across financial services for clarity, allowing you to better understand what you're paying for and how those fees affect your trust's bottom line. Hidden fees can quickly erode returns, and being oblivious to them is no longer an option. Demanding transparency from your financial advisors and trust managers allows you to gain valuable insight, leading to more efficient management of your trust. Knowing exactly where your money is going helps in negotiating better fee structures and ensuring that every dollar serves its purpose efficiently.

Diversification Practices

Asset diversification remains a hallmark strategy for maintaining financial security and optimizing returns. Diversifying across different markets or products can reduce risk and enhance the performance of your estate over time. Meanwhile, understanding performance monitoring techniques helps ensure your assets are growing according to plan, meeting the goals set in your estate plan. This practice not only safeguards your trust's holdings against market fluctuations but also enhances resilience, ensuring that not all investments are adversely affected at the same time. A well-diversified portfolio acts as a financial safety net, providing peace of mind that your estate will maintain its value even amidst instability.

Performance Monitoring Techniques

Performance monitoring techniques have also evolved significantly. Today, there are innovative tools and technologies available that provide real-time data and analytics on how investments are performing. Access to this level of detail allows you to make proactive adjustments to your portfolio, ensuring it remains aligned with your financial goals. For instance, using dashboard apps that consolidate all trust-related finances can help monitor performance metrics at a glance. Such tools encourage continuous assessment and refinement of strategies, ensuring your investments remain on a profitable path and adapt to any emerging trends or potential risks.

As you navigate these evolving practices, it's essential to remember that every trust is unique, with its own goals and constraints. Customizing your approach according to these changes requires patience, expertise, and willingness to adapt. When exploring new investment strategies or seeking fee transparency, consulting with knowledgeable advisors can ensure you stay on track.

Keeping abreast of these developments empowers you to make informed decisions. By doing so, you not only enhance your financial strategy but also safeguard your trust's future. You are in the driver's seat to maximize your returns and ensure the longevity of your estate.

Looking forward, it's apparent that technological advancements will continue to shape estate planning in innovative ways, which we'll discuss next. Digital tools and platforms are simplifying various estate planning processes, making them more accessible and manageable. In a world where technology accelerates change, integrating these tools will prove paramount. We will explore these technological trends and their implications for modern estate planning, discovering how they can make the process more efficient and effective for everyone involved.

Impact of Technology on Estate Planning Part 1

In estate planning, we've already discussed the changing financial practices that reflect broader shifts in strategy and transparency. Now, let's look at how these changes helped the field accept the powerful effects of technology.

Online Estate Planning Tools

First, consider online estate planning tools. These digital platforms have democratized the process, especially for those with limited resources. They strip away complexity, making it accessible for anyone to draft living trusts. Think of platforms like Willful or Trust & Will, where a few clicks replace hours in a lawyer's office. These tools not only simplify the creation of legal documents but do so at a fraction of traditional costs. Offering templates and guided instructions ensures users can navigate complex information with ease, providing clarity without requiring them to decode legal jargon. But this ease-of-use merely scratches the surface of their potential. The real innovation lies in how they integrate with broader digital ecosystems, linking users to other financial tools and offering a holistic picture of assets.

Digital Record Keeping

As we transition from simplicity to security, digital record-keeping becomes paramount. Secure tech solutions help protect important information. Utilizing cloud storage services like Google Drive or specialized platforms such as Everplans, estate planners can safeguard documents electronically. But storage is just one part of the equation. The conversation must extend to security measures like encryption and multi-factor authentication that prevent unauthorized access. Organizing and protecting estate documents digitally helps planners reduce physical clutter while minimizing the risks associated with hard copies, ensuring that critical information remains both accessible and secure.

Impact of Blockchain Technology

Blockchain technology, as it emerges in this arena, changes the game by redefining trust and transparency in estate documentation. At its core, blockchain ensures an immutable record, a feature that makes it particularly appealing for estate planners seeking to enhance trust management. Imagine a scenario where the transfer of assets or the verification of trusts occurs on a blockchain network, leaving an indelible mark that can be traced but never altered. While still emerging, blockchain applications in estate planning invite us to imagine a world where technological confidence reduces disputes and heightens transparency.

Artificial Intelligence in Estate Planning

Artificial Intelligence (AI) rounds out our exploration by adding a personalized touch to estate planning. AI tools assess individual circumstances, processing vast amounts of data to provide tailored advice. Tools like Wealthfront and Betterment use AI to customize financial strategies, aiming for the same precision in estate planning. As AI analyzes user data, it determines optimal approaches to managing and distributing estates, factoring in unique needs and constraints. This level of personalization resonates with those eager for bespoke financial strategies without the premium price tag. AI's potential reaches further as it continues to learn, evolving its recommendations with changing personal or legal landscapes.

These individual technologies combine to transform the estate planning landscape, each offering unique insights and opportunities. Online tools democratize access, digital record-keeping intensifies security, blockchain fosters trust, and AI personalizes the journey. These innovations create a new way of planning estates that meets modern needs and expectations, moving from a one-size-fits-all approach to one that is as diverse as the people it serves.

Given these remarkable advances, it's natural to wonder where technology will take us next. As we move to future estate planning trends, consider the increased personalization that emerging technologies suggest. What might the next stage of AI tell us about our estates? How will blockchain redefine our legal frameworks? These are questions that provoke not only curiosity but anticipation for a future where estate planning becomes not just a legal necessity but an integral element of our lives, effortlessly tailored to our evolving circumstances.

Impact of Technology on Estate Planning: Part 2

Estate planning is undergoing a transformation as technology plays an increasingly significant role. Emerging trends indicate a future where personalization in trusts becomes standard practice, with AI and blockchain revolutionizing the management of assets. A living trust that adapts to real-time financial changes is no longer a far-fetched idea—AI-driven algorithms can manage assets based on shifting market conditions, individual priorities, or lifestyle adjustments. The result is a dynamic estate plan that evolves to better serve beneficiaries over time.

Evolving Legal Frameworks

As estate planning incorporates more technology, legal frameworks will need to evolve accordingly. Existing laws may not sufficiently account for digital assets such as cryptocurrencies, non-fungible tokens, and online businesses. Without precise legal structures, these assets risk being excluded from traditional estate plans.

Future legal adjustments will likely mandate the inclusion and protection of digital assets in estate documents. This ensures that an individual's entire portfolio—including virtual investments—is properly documented and transferred without complications.

Smart Contracts and Automated Estate Execution

Technology-driven solutions such as **smart contracts** can significantly simplify estate executions. These digital agreements **automatically enforce estate distribution** once predetermined conditions are met, removing the need for lengthy court procedures.

Smart contracts offer several advantages:

- **Reduced administrative burden** by automating asset distribution.
- **Minimized legal fees** as processes become more efficient.
- **Expedited estate settlements**, ensuring beneficiaries receive assets without unnecessary delays.

This modernization of estate planning helps grieving families navigate financial transitions with fewer legal obstacles.

Personalization Through AI and Advanced Analytics

Estate planning has traditionally been a rigid process, but AI introduces adaptive strategies that enhance flexibility. You can have a trust that modifies spending allocations based on a beneficiary's employment status, financial needs, or health conditions. AI-driven tools can tailor estate plans in a way that ensures support arrives at the right time and in the right form.

AI also aids estate planners in forecasting long-term impacts. Analyzing trends and generating scenario-based outcomes transforms estate planning into a proactive strategy, ensuring it evolves with financial and legal changes rather than remaining a static document requiring frequent revisions.

Integrating AI for Efficiency in Estate Management

Technology not only enhances personalization but also streamlines estate planning. AI can automate repetitive tasks such as:

- **Asset classification**, ensuring investments are properly documented.
- **Tax estimations**, making financial calculations more accurate.

This automation allows estate planners to focus on strategic decision-making rather than administrative tasks, improving the efficiency and precision of estate management

Embracing the Future of Estate Planning

With technological advancements and legal changes reshaping estate strategies, adapting to these trends is essential. Estate plans must reflect modern financial landscapes, ensuring they remain relevant and effective for future generations.

Preparing for these changes ensures that financial legacies are preserved while facilitating smoother estate transfers. Staying informed and adaptable allows estate planners and families to navigate complexities with confidence, aligning estate structures with long-term goals and values.

The possibilities are revolutionary. Technology enhances efficiency, legal adaptations improve inclusivity, and family-centered approaches foster unity in estate planning.

Examining how estate strategies can adjust to future developments is essential for effective planning. Rather than simply reacting to changes, preparing in advance ensures a smooth and adaptable approach that aligns with evolving financial and legal landscapes.

Future Predictions for Estate Planning Practices

As we transition from exploring technologies like blockchain and AI, it's clear that these innovations lay the groundwork for shifts in estate planning. These technologies are the catalysts for change. Blockchain ensures transactions are secure and transparent, something crucial in estate documentation. AI, meanwhile, offers predictability and efficiency, potentially forecasting financial trends or flagging vital patterns in estate management. Together, these technologies offer a sneak peek into future estate planning practices.

Increased Personalization in Trusts

Now, let's consider where these innovations could take us. Imagine smarter trusts tailored to individual needs. Personalized trusts can adapt not just to financial situations but to family dynamics. For example, a trust could be structured to help a minor through college or support a family business as it adapts to market changes. Such customization ensures that estate planning isn't static but dynamic and in tune with the beneficiaries' evolving needs.

Evolving Legal Frameworks

In terms of legal frameworks, we're likely heading towards more adaptive laws in estate planning. Currently, legal jargon and outdated regulations can obstruct rather than aid understanding. Let's envisage a shift where laws become more intuitive, with user-friendly language making them accessible. Imagine governments introducing flexible legislation allowing people to make real-time adjustments to wills and trusts as circumstances change. Say a person transfers assets seamlessly across borders with laws that simplify such processes.

Technological Integration in Estate Plans

Technology could also simplify documentation, which is a notoriously complex part of estate planning. Think of virtual tools or apps, that provide instant access to essential documents with secure cloud storage. These tools might guide users through drafting and updating a will or trust, simplifying legal consultations by integrating AI to answer basic queries instantly. Consider an app that nudges you to update your estate plans whenever there's a significant life event—a marriage, birth, or career change. This convenience ensures plans reflect real-life changes.

Intergenerational Planning Trends

Intergenerational planning is another area poised for evolution. We often underestimate the importance of cross-generational dialogue in estate planning. Families may avoid discussing inheritances until it's too late, causing conflict and confusion. Enter technology: imagine virtual family meeting spaces where even distant relatives could participate in discussions and decision-making. Such platforms could host topics like sustainable asset management, ensuring that environmental consciousness is part of the estate-planning discourse.

Family conversations could also benefit from AI-driven insights into family dynamics. Ever wondered if there's a science to estate planning? AI could analyze communication styles and offer strategies to mediate conflicts. Picture AI algorithms analyzing patterns and suggesting optimal ways to introduce certain topics or financial concepts based on family discussions. This not only aids harmony but also encourages proactive planning.

Let's dig a bit deeper into these speculative trends. Picture a scenario where biometric security tools help safeguard assets, much like a sci-fi movie plot where only recognized fingerprints or voice commands can authorize transactions. Biometric tools could ensure an extra layer of security, instilling confidence as power of attorney is exercised or trust funds are allocated.

Further, estate planning may also embrace emerging technologies like augmented reality (AR). Imagine exploring a virtual representation of entire estate plans. Through AR, families could visualize assets, how they'll be distributed, and even simulate future financial scenarios. This kind of immersion transforms an abstract idea into a tangible reality.

Predicting future trends wouldn't be complete without considering global shifts. With climate change at the forefront, there's potential for estate planning to include green clauses or sustainability conditions. An example might be an agreement that ensures investments adhere to eco-friendly principles or implementing green burial options. These considerations align estate planning with broader ethical and global expectations.

It's important to highlight that none of these advancements eliminate the human element of estate planning. While tech simplifies many processes, personal reflection and conversations remain pivotal. No tool or algorithm can replace the significance of expressing personal values and hopes for the future. Estate planning underlines the importance of defining what legacy someone wishes to leave behind.

On a broader financial scope, the rise of cryptocurrencies and alternative assets are disrupting traditional estate considerations. A future estate plan might feature crypto holdings or digital art collections, creating dialogue about how these unconventional assets are valued and transferred. Imagine a world where digital assets hold equal weight as real estate, making wills far more inclusive of modern wealth.

As these trends begin to converge, the accessibility of estate planning will likely broaden. Traditionally, estate planning catered to those with ample resources, often alienating those with limited financial means. Innovations could democratize access; start-ups might offer free consultation services online, or payment plans tailored for economically diverse individuals.

The future estate planners are skilled with technology and understand people's feelings, which makes them more than just legal advisors. They need to combine compassion with tech skills while considering future needs and current situations.

These predictions are realistic advancements in estate planning, not distant possibilities. Personalization, legal adaptability, technology, and intergenerational communication are shaping the future. Staying informed about these trends allows individuals to plan effectively rather than just respond to changes.

Concluding Thoughts

As we've explored the impact of recent legal updates on trusts, it's clear that staying informed is key to navigating these changes effectively. Now that we know these updates influence everything from trust duration and beneficiary provisions to tax obligations and trustee duties, we can proactively adjust our estate plans to safeguard our assets and honor our intentions. Being involved and flexible isn't just about keeping up—it's about creating a future that ensures your success and meets today's needs.

In the next chapter, we'll outline the essential documents needed to create a living trust, ensuring legal clarity and a well-structured estate plan.

Chapter 15: Essential Documents

While the concept of a trust itself provides a structured way to safeguard wealth and minimize legal complications, the process of building one requires careful documentation at various stages. Every form serves a distinct purpose, whether it's establishing trust, transferring assets, or defining beneficiaries, and missing a key document could lead to unnecessary challenges down the road.

This chapter will break down the essential documents needed to construct a living trust, explaining their specific roles and when each is required. From the initial Declaration of Trust, which formally establishes the trust, to the Asset Transfer Documents that assign property to the trust, each stage involves critical paperwork that ensures legal validity and clarity. Understanding these documents will empower you to create a well-structured trust, avoid common pitfalls, and ensure your estate plan remains aligned with your long-term goals.

Revocable Living Trust

A revocable living trust is a flexible estate planning tool that allows individuals to manage and distribute their assets efficiently while avoiding probate. It provides control over wealth during one's lifetime and ensures a seamless transfer of assets upon death.

Why Use a Revocable Living Trust?

A revocable living trust offers several key advantages, making it a preferred option for estate planning:

1. **Avoids Probate:** Unlike a will, assets placed in a trust do not go through probate, ensuring a faster and more private distribution process.

2. **Maintains Control:** The creator of the trust (grantor) retains full authority over the assets while alive, allowing modifications or cancellations at any time.

3. **Provides for Incapacity:** If the grantor becomes incapacitated, a successor trustee can manage the assets, avoiding court-appointed guardianship.

4. **Ensures Privacy:** Probate records are public, whereas trusts remain confidential, protecting sensitive financial details.

5. **Simplifies Asset Distribution:** Clearly outlines how assets are distributed, reducing disputes among beneficiaries.

When Should You Establish a Revocable Living Trust?

Setting up a trust depends on individual circumstances, but common scenarios where it is beneficial include:

- **Preparing for the Future:** Ideal for individuals who want a structured plan for asset management if they become incapacitated or pass away.

- **Avoiding Probate Hassles:** Particularly useful in states with lengthy probate processes or high probate fees.

- **Protecting Beneficiaries:** Beneficial for minors or financially inexperienced heirs who need structured inheritance management.

- **Owning Multiple Properties:** Helps streamline the transfer of real estate assets in different states, bypassing separate probate procedures.

- **Ensuring Smooth Business Succession:** Allows business owners to transition ownership efficiently upon death or incapacity.

How to Set Up and Use a Revocable Living Trust

1. **Choose a Trustee:**
    - Select a trustworthy individual or institution to manage assets if you become unable to do so.
    - You can be the trustee while alive, with a successor trustee stepping in upon incapacity or death.
2. **Create the Trust Document:**
    - Work with an estate planning attorney to draft the legal document outlining beneficiaries, trustees, and asset distribution instructions.
    - Ensure the document is comprehensive, specifying all conditions for asset management.
3. **Transfer Assets into the Trust:**
    - Change the ownership or title of assets like bank accounts, properties, and investments to reflect the trust as the owner.
    - Assets not transferred into the trust will still go through probate.
4. **Regularly Review and Update:**
    - Modify terms as financial circumstances or family situations change.
    - Add new assets or adjust beneficiary instructions to align with evolving estate goals.
5. **Distribute Assets Upon Death:**
    - The successor trustee follows the trust's guidelines to distribute assets with-

out court interference.

- Trust administration is **more efficient** than probate, ensuring heirs receive assets faster.

A revocable living trust streamlines estate planning, offering control, privacy, and efficiency in asset management. Setting it up early prevents probate complications, ensures a smooth transition for heirs, and provides financial security in case of incapacity. Transferring assets properly into the trust is important to maximize its benefits.

Revocable Living Trust Template

This Revocable Living Trust is made this________ [Date], by and between:

Grantor (Settlor):

Full Legal Name: ____

Address: ____

Phone Number: ____

Email Address (Optional): ____

Trustee (Initial trustee of the trust):

Full Legal Name: ____

Address: ____

Phone Number:____

Email Address (Optional): ____

Successor Trustee (In case the initial trustee is unavailable):

Full Legal Name: ____

Address: ____

Phone Number: ____

Email Address (Optional): ____

1. Declaration of Trust

I, ________________________ [Grantor's Full Name], the undersigned Grantor, hereby create and establish this Revocable Living Trust (the "Trust"), which shall be governed by the following terms and conditions. The primary purpose of this Trust is to provide for the management of my assets during my lifetime and to distribute those assets upon my death without the need for probate.

2. Appointment of Trustee

I hereby appoint ________________________ [Trustee's Full Name] as the Trustee of this Trust. If ________________________[Trustee's Full Name] is unable or unwilling to serve as Trustee, I appoint ________________________ [Successor Trustee's Full Name] as Successor Trustee to manage the Trust in accordance with the terms of this document.

3. Funding of the Trust

The assets of this Trust shall consist of any property transferred to it by me during my lifetime or upon my death. A schedule of the assets currently held in the Trust is attached hereto as **Exhibit A**. These assets may include, but are not limited to, real property, bank accounts, securities, and other personal property.

4. Powers of the Trustee

The Trustee shall have the following powers in connection with the administration of the Trust, in addition to those otherwise conferred by law or custom:

- To buy, sell, lease, or manage property of any kind;
- To invest and reinvest Trust assets in any legal investment, including but not limited to real estate, stocks, bonds, and mutual funds;

- To borrow money on behalf of the Trust and pledge Trust assets as collateral if necessary;
- To make distributions to the Beneficiaries as provided in this Trust;
- To pay any taxes, expenses, or debts of the Trust from Trust assets;
- To employ attorneys, accountants, and other professionals for assistance with Trust administration.

5. Distributions of Trust Assets During the Grantor's Lifetime

While I am alive and mentally competent, I shall retain full control over the Trust assets. I may withdraw or transfer assets from the Trust at any time and for any purpose. During my lifetime, the Trustee shall distribute the Trust's income and principal in accordance with my instructions or as I may direct from time to time.

6. Distribution of Trust Assets Upon the Grantor's Death

Upon my death, the Trustee shall distribute the assets of the Trust as follows:

- To my spouse, _______________ [Spouse's Full Name], if they survive me, the sum of $ _______ [Amount] or _______ [Percentage]% of the Trust assets, in addition to any property they may be entitled to under the terms of our marital property agreement or applicable law.
- To my children, ________________________________ [Children's Full Names], equally, or in the following proportions:
    -
    -
    -
    - If any child predeceases me, their share will pass to their descendants, per stirpes.

If I have not designated specific beneficiaries for certain assets, I direct the Trustee to distribute those assets in equal shares to my surviving children or as otherwise directed in a separate document or codicil to this Trust.

7. Successor Trustee

In the event of my death or incapacity, the Successor Trustee, ______________ [Successor Trustee's Full Name], shall assume responsibility for managing and distributing the Trust assets as provided in this document. If the Successor Trustee is unable or unwilling to serve, I appoint ____________________ [Alternate Successor Trustee's Full Name] to serve in their place.

8. Incapacity of the Grantor

If I become incapacitated, as determined by a licensed physician, the Successor Trustee shall manage the Trust for my benefit and distribute Trust assets as necessary to provide for my care and well-being. The Successor Trustee shall have full authority to act on my behalf, as specified in this document

9. Trustee's Powers in Case of Incapacity

If I am unable to manage my financial affairs due to incapacity, the Trustee shall have the power to manage my assets in accordance with my best interests and as provided in this Trust. This may include paying for my medical expenses, housing, and other care-related costs.

10. Trustee's Compensation

The Trustee is entitled to reasonable compensation for their services in managing the Trust. The compensation will be determined based on the time spent and the complexity of the tasks involved. If the Trustee is a family member, they may choose to serve without compensation, unless otherwise specified in this document.

11. Revocation and Amendment of the Trust

I retain the right to revoke or amend this Trust at any time during my lifetime. Any such revocation or amendment must be made in writing and executed in the same manner as the original Trust document.

12. Special Instructions for Specific Assets

The following are my specific instructions for the distribution of certain assets upon my death:

• **Real Property:**

____ [Description of any specific real property and how it should be handled or distributed].

• **Personal Property:**

____

[Description of specific personal property, such as family heirlooms, vehicles, etc., and instructions for distribution].

14. Governing Law

This Trust is governed by the laws of the State of __________ [State], and any disputes regarding the Trust shall be resolved under the jurisdiction of the courts in __________ [County], __________ [State].

15. Miscellaneous Provisions

• **Spendthrift Clause**: The assets in the Trust shall not be subject to the claims of creditors or any beneficiary's creditors.

• **No Contest Clause**: If any beneficiary contests the terms of this Trust, they shall forfeit their share of the Trust

Signatures and Execution

Grantor's Signature: ___________________________

Date: ___________________________

Trustee's Signature: ___________________________

Date: ___________________________

Witnesses (if required)

Witness 1's Signature: ___________________________

Date: ___________________________

Witness 2's Signature: ___________________________

Date: ___________________________

Notary Public (if required)

State of ____________ [State] County of ___________ [County] On this ____________ [Date], before me, a Notary Public, personally appeared ____________________ [Grantor's Full Name], known to me to be the person whose name is subscribed to this instrument and acknowledged that ______ [he/she] executed the same for the purposes therein contained.

Notary Public Signature: ___________________________

Date: ___________________________

Assignment of Personal Property

An Assignment of Personal Property is an essential estate planning document that formally transfers ownership of personal belongings into a trust. Items such as furniture, jewelry, collectibles, and keepsakes are included, ensuring they are managed according to the trust's directives rather than going through probate.

Why Use an Assignment of Personal Property?

This document provides several key benefits:

- **Ensures Proper Inclusion in the Trust:** Without it, personal belongings may not be covered, leading to probate issues.
- **Avoids Legal Uncertainty:** Establishes clear ownership of items under the trust, preventing disputes.
- **Simplifies Estate Administration:** Makes asset distribution more efficient for trustees and beneficiaries.
- **Protects Sentimental and Valuable Items:** Ensures that specific belongings are transferred to intended recipients.

When Should You Complete This Assignment?

It's best to finalize the assignment shortly after the trust is created, ensuring that personal property is fully included in estate planning. Common reasons for completing this step include:

- **Establishing a new trust** and needing to transfer assets promptly.
- **Updating an existing trust** to reflect new acquisitions or changing beneficiaries.
- **Minimizing probate complications** by ensuring every asset is documented under the trust.

How to Execute an Assignment of Personal Property

1. **List Covered Items:**
    - Identify personal belongings to be transferred, ensuring clarity on valuable and sentimental assets.
2. **Prepare the Assignment Document:**
    - Draft a formal legal document specifying items being assigned to the trust.
    - Ensure clear descriptions to avoid ambiguity in ownership transfers.
3. **Sign and Date the Document:**
    - The trust grantor must sign and date the assignment to validate the transfer.
    - A notary may be required in some cases for additional legal confirmation.
4. **Attach to the Trust Agreement:**
    - Include the document with the trust records, ensuring trustees can reference it during estate administration.
5. **Update as Needed:**
    - Make modifications to reflect new assets or changes in personal belongings over time.

An Assignment of Personal Property ensures that personal belongings are legally transferred into a trust, preventing probate issues and simplifying asset management. Completing this document early and keeping it updated helps secure valuable and sentimental assets, making estate administration efficient and conflict-free.

Assignment of Personal Property

This ASSIGNMENT OF PERSONAL PROPERTY is made on _______ [Date], by and between:

Grantor (Assignor):

- Full Legal Name: ______________________________
- Address: ______________________________
- Phone Number: ______________________________
- Email Address (optional): ______________________________

Assignee (Recipient):

- Full Legal Name: ______________________________
- Address: ______________________________
- Phone Number: ______________________________
- Email Address (optional): ______________________________

1. Introduction

I, ________________ [Grantor's Full Name], hereby assign, transfer, and convey to ________________ [Assignee's Full Name], the following personal property, to be held and managed by the Assignee for the purposes described in this Agreement. This transfer is made under the terms set forth below.

2. Description of Personal Property

The personal property being assigned to the Assignee is as follows:

Item 1:

- Description: ______________________________
- Estimated Value: $____________________

- Serial Number (if applicable): ____________________
- Condition: [New/Used/Good/Excellent/Other]
- Transfer Date: ____________________

Item 2:

- Description: ______________________________
- Estimated Value: $____________________
- Serial Number (if applicable): ____________________
- Condition: [New/Used/Good/Excellent/Other]
- Transfer Date: ____________________

Item 3:

- Description: ______________________________
- Estimated Value: $____________________
- Serial Number (if applicable): ____________________
- Condition: [New/Used/Good/Excellent/Other]
- Transfer Date: ____________________
- (Add additional items as necessary)

3. Purpose of the Assignment

The purpose of this assignment is to transfer ownership of the listed personal property to the Assignee for the following purpose(s):

- ______________________________
- ______________________________
- ______________________________

4. No Retention of Interest by Grantor

Upon execution of this Assignment, I, the Grantor, have transferred all rights, title, and interest in the listed personal property to the Assignee. I will retain no further interest or control over the property, except as may be expressly stated in this Agreement.

5. Representations and Warranties of the Grantor

I represent and warrant that:

- I am the sole and legal owner of the listed personal property.
- The property is free from any encumbrances, liens, or claims of any kind.
- I have full authority to transfer the property to the Assignee.
- The property is being transferred in its current condition, as described in the "Condition" section.

6. Acceptance by the Assignee

The Assignee hereby acknowledges receipt of the personal property listed above and agrees to assume all responsibility for the care, maintenance, and management of the property from the date of this Assignment. The Assignee further agrees to:

- Keep the property in good condition and maintain insurance on the property, if applicable.
- Not sell, lease, or dispose of the property without the prior written consent of the Grantor (if applicable).
- Use the property only for the purposes outlined in this Agreement.

7. Liability and Indemnification

The Assignee agrees to indemnify and hold harmless the Grantor from any liability, loss, or damages arising out of the Assignee's possession or use of the property, except in cases of fraud, gross negligence, or willful misconduct.

8. Termination of Assignment

This Assignment shall remain in effect unless terminated by mutual written agreement of the Grantor and Assignee or by operation of law. Upon termination, the property shall be returned to the Grantor, unless otherwise agreed.

9. Governing Law

This Assignment shall be governed by and construed in accordance with the laws of the State of __________ [State], without regard to its conflict of laws principles.

10. Miscellaneous Provisions

- **Entire Agreement:** This document constitutes the entire agreement between the parties regarding the transfer of personal property and supersedes any prior discussions or agreements.
- **Amendments:** Any amendments to this Agreement must be in writing and signed by both the Grantor and Assignee.
- **Severability:** If any provision of this Assignment is found to be invalid or unenforceable, the remainder of the Assignment will remain in full force and effect.

Signatures:

Grantor's Signature: ____________________________

Date: ____________________________

Assignee's Signature: ____________________________

Date: ____________________________

Witnesses (if applicable)

Witness 1's Signature: ___________________________

Date: ___________________________

Witness 2's Signature: ___________________________

Date: ___________________________

Notary Public (if required)

State of ___________ [State]

County of __________ [County]

On this _________ [Date], before me, a Notary Public, personally appeared _________________ [Grantor's Full Name] and _________________ [Assignee's Full Name], known to me to be the persons whose names are subscribed to this document and acknowledged that they executed the same for the purposes therein contained.

Notary's Signature: ___________________________

Date: ___________________________

Schedule of Trust Assets

A Schedule of Trust Assets is an essential document that lists all assets transferred into a trust. It serves as a record of ownership, ensuring trustees can manage these assets effectively and preventing disputes or confusion about what the trust controls.

Why Use a Schedule of Trust Assets?

This document provides several key benefits:

- **Defines Trust Ownership:** Clearly establishes which assets belong to the trust, avoiding ambiguity.
- **Helps Trustees Manage Assets:** Provides an accurate reference for asset distribution and financial planning.
- **Prevents Probate Complications:** Ensures that all listed assets remain within the trust, avoiding unnecessary probate proceedings.
- **Keeps Estate Planning Organized:** Allows for systematic tracking and updating of trust assets over time.

When Should You Create and Update a Schedule of Trust Assets?

A Schedule of Trust Assets should be completed as soon as you begin funding your trust. Regular updates are necessary when:

- **New assets** are acquired and need to be transferred into the trust.
- **Existing trust assets** are sold, replaced, or reallocated.
- **Trust ownership needs clarification** due to changes in financial plans or estate updates.

How to Prepare a Schedule of Trust Assets?

1. **List All Transferred Assets:**
   - Include real estate, bank accounts, investments, vehicles, business interests, and personal valuables.
2. **Provide Detailed Descriptions:**
   - Specify asset names, values, account numbers, and locations to ensure accuracy.
3. **Attach Supporting Documents:**
   - Include titles, deeds, account statements, and ownership certificates to verify asset transfer.
4. **Sign and Date the Schedule:**
   - Ensure that the document is legally recognized and attached to trust records.
5. **Update the Schedule Regularly:**
   - Revise entries whenever new assets are added, removed, or restructured.

A well-maintained Schedule of Trust Assets enhances trust management and ensures a clear, organized estate plan, allowing for smooth asset distribution and financial oversight.

Schedule of Trust Assets

This Schedule of Trust Assets is an integral part of the ________________ [Trust Name] Revocable Living Trust, dated ______________ [Date of Trust], and lists all assets currently transferred to the Trust by ____________________ [Grantor's Full Name], the undersigned Grantor.

1. **Real Property**

Property 1:

- Property Address: ____
- Legal Description: ____
- Estimated Value: $______________________
- Transferred to Trust: [Yes/No]
- Transfer Date: ________________________
- Ownership Type: [Sole Ownership, Joint Ownership, etc.]

Property 2:

- Property Address: ____
- Legal Description: ____
- Estimated Value: $________
- Transferred to Trust: [Yes/No]
- Transfer Date: ________________________

2. **Bank Accounts**

Account 1:

- Bank Name: ______________________________________
- Account Type: [Checking/Savings/Other]
- Account Number (Last 4 Digits): ________________________
- Estimated Value: $____________________
- Transferred to Trust: [Yes/No]
- Transfer Date: ____________________

Account 2:

- Bank Name: ______________________
- Account Type: [Checking/Savings/Other]
- Account Number (Last 4 Digits): ________________________
- Estimated Value: $____________________
- Transferred to Trust: [Yes/No]
- Transfer Date: ____________________

3. **Securities and Investments**

Investment 1:

- Name of Security: ______________________________________
- Number of Shares: ____________________
- Estimated Value: $____________________
- Transferred to Trust: [Yes/No]
- Transfer Date: ____________________

Investment 2:

- Name of Security: ______________________________________
- Number of Shares: ____________________
- Estimated Value: $____________________
- Transferred to Trust: [Yes/No]
- Transfer Date: ____________________

4. **Personal Property**

Item 1:

- Description of Property:
  ____
- Estimated Value: $____________________
- Transferred to Trust: [Yes/No]
- Transfer Date: ____________________

Item 2:

- Description of Property:
  ____
- Estimated Value: $____________________
- Transferred to Trust: [Yes/No]
- Transfer Date: ____________________

5. Life Insurance Policies

Policy 1:

- Insurance Company:
  ____
- Policy Number: ______________________
- Face Value: $____________________
- Beneficiary: [Trust Name]
- Transferred to Trust: [Yes/No]
- Transfer Date: ____________________

Policy 2:

- Insurance Company:
  ____
- Policy Number: ______________________
- Face Value: $____________________
- Beneficiary: [Trust Name]
- Transferred to Trust: [Yes/No]
- Transfer Date: ____________________

6. **Business Interests**

Business 1:

- Business Name: ____________________
- Nature of Business: ____________________
- Ownership Percentage: ____________________
- Estimated Value: $____________________
- Transferred to Trust: [Yes/No]
- Transfer Date: ____________________

Business 2:

- Business Name: ____________________
- Nature of Business: ____________________
- Ownership Percentage: ____________________
- Estimated Value: $____________________
- Transferred to Trust: [Yes/No]
- Transfer Date: ____________________

7. **Miscellaneous Assets**

Asset 1:

- Description of Asset: ____________________
- Estimated Value: $____________________
- Transferred to Trust: [Yes/No]
- Transfer Date: ____________________

Asset 2:

- Description of Asset: ____________________
- Estimated Value: $____________________

- Transferred to Trust: [Yes/No]
- Transfer Date: ____________________

8. **Total Value of Trust Assets**
   The total estimated value of the assets listed above is:
   $____________________

9. **Trustee's Acknowledgment**

I, ____________________[Trustee's Full Name], as Trustee of the ____________________ [Trust Name] Revocable Living Trust, confirm that I have reviewed and acknowledge the assets listed in this Schedule of Trust Assets, and I will manage these assets in accordance with the provisions of the Trust Agreement.

Trustee's Signature: ____________________
Date: ____________________

Pour-Over Will

A Pour-Over Will acts as a backup plan for estate management, ensuring that any assets not transferred into a trust during your lifetime are directed there after death. This guarantees that the trust remains the primary governing document for asset distribution.

Why Use a Pour-Over Will?

This document provides several essential benefits:

- **Captures Unassigned Assets:** Any belongings not formally placed into the trust are transferred after death.
- **Ensures Consistency in Estate Planning:** Keeps all assets under the trust's management rather than being separately handled through probate.
- **Minimizes Probate Complexity:** Though assets must go through probate before being transferred, it ensures they reach the trust rather than being distributed according to standard probate rules.
- **Prevents Legal Gaps:** Ensures no assets are unintentionally excluded from the trust's protection.

When Should You Create a Pour-Over Will?

A Pour-Over Will should be established simultaneously with a living trust to ensure proper estate planning coverage.It is particularly beneficial when:

- **New assets** are acquired and not immediately transferred into the trust.
- **Oversights occur** where some possessions are unintentionally left outside the trust.
- **Estate planning updates** require adjustments to asset management strategies.

How to Set Up and Use a Pour-Over Will

1. **Draft the Document Alongside the Trust:**
    - Clearly specify that any unassigned assets should be transferred into the trust.
2. **List Applicable Assets:**
    - Identify potential items that may need to be transferred to the trust upon death.
3. **Ensure Legal Validity:**
    - The will should meet state legal requirements, including proper witnessing and notarization.
4. **Coordinate with Trust Documents:**
    - Review the trust regularly to minimize reliance on the Pour-Over Will.
5. **Update as Necessary:**
    - Adjust asset lists and trust details based on new acquisitions or estate planning changes.

A Pour-Over Will serves as a safeguard, ensuring that all assets, even those unintentionally left out, are integrated into the trust's management for seamless estate administration.

Pour Over Will

THIS POUR-OVER WILL is made this [Date], by and between:

Testator (Principal):

- Full Legal Name: ______________________________
- Address: ______________________________
- Phone Number: ______________________________
- Email Address (optional): ______________________________

1. **Declaration of Testator**

   I, ____________________ [Principal's Full Name], being of sound mind and disposing memory, do hereby declare this to be my Last Will and Testament. I revoke all prior wills and codicils made by me.

2. **Appointment of Executor**

   I appoint ____________________ [Executor's Full Name], residing at ______________________________________ [Executor's Address], as the Executor of my estate. If ____________________ [Executor's Full Name] is unable or unwilling to serve, I appoint ____________________ [Alternate Executor's Full Name], residing at [Alternate Executor's Address], as the successor Executor.

3. **Appointment of Guardian for Minor Children (if applicable)**

   If I have minor children at the time of my death, I appoint ____________________ [Guardian's Full Name], residing at ______________________________________ [Guardian's Address], as the guardian of my minor children. If ____________________ [Guardian's Full Name] is unable or unwilling to serve, I appoint

____________________ [Alternate Guardian's Full Name], residing at ____ [Alternate Guardian's Address], as the successor guardian.

4. Pour-Over Provision

I direct that all property, real or personal, not already placed in my ______________ [Trust Name] Revocable Living Trust, dated ________ [Date of Trust], be transferred upon my death to the Trustee of that Trust, to be added to the Trust and administered in accordance with the terms of the Trust. The assets transferred to the Trust shall be distributed to my designated beneficiaries as outlined in the Trust Agreement.

5. Specific Bequests (if applicable)

I make the following specific bequests:

- To ____________________ [Beneficiary's Full Name], I give and bequeath ______________________ [Specific Item or Property, e.g., "my diamond ring" or "my collection of first-edition books"].

- To ________________________ [Beneficiary's Full Name], I give and bequeath the sum of $[Amount] for their use and benefit.

6. Residual Estate

All property not specifically bequeathed under this Will, or not transferred to my Trust, shall be distributed as follows:

- To ___________________ [Beneficiary's Full Name], I give and bequeath [Percentage]% of the residue of my estate.

- To ____________________ [Beneficiary's Full Name], I give and bequeath [Percentage]% of the residue of my estate.

If any beneficiary predeceases me, their share shall be distributed to their descendants, per stirpes.

7. Revocation of Previous Wills and Codicils

I hereby revoke all previous wills and codicils executed by me. This Will is my last will and testament and supersedes any prior documents.

8. Executor's Powers

I give my Executor the following powers and duties:

- To collect and manage my estate's assets, pay debts, and distribute property as instructed in this Will.
- To liquidate assets if necessary and distribute funds to the designated beneficiaries.
- To hire professionals, such as attorneys, accountants, or financial advisors, as needed for the administration of my estate.

9. No Contest Clause (optional)

If any beneficiary under this Will or any person who claims through them contests this Will or any part of it and the contest is unsuccessful, they shall forfeit any and all benefits under this Will.

10. Disposition of Remains

I express my preference regarding the disposition of my remains as follows:

- [Choice 1: Cremation, Burial, etc.]
- [Additional instructions regarding the funeral, memorial, or other services]

11.Signatures and Witnessing

This Will is executed by me, __________________ [Testator's Full Name], on this ________ [Date], in the presence of the undersigned witnesses, who affirm that I signed this Will voluntarily and with full understanding of its contents.

Testator's Signature: ____________________________

Date: ____________________________

12.Witnesses

We, the undersigned witnesses, hereby affirm that on the date above written, ____________________ [Testator's Full Name] signed this Will in our presence and that they appeared to be of sound mind and not under duress.

Witness 1's Signature: ____________________________
Date: ____________________________

Witness 2's Signature: ____________________________
Date: ____________________________

13.Notary Public (if applicable)

State of _________ [State] County of ____________ [County] On this __________ [Date], before me, a Notary Public, personally appeared _______________ [Testator's Full Name], known to me or provided identification, and acknowledged that they signed this document as their free and voluntary act.

Notary Public Signature: ___________________________
Date: __________________________

Durable Power of Attorney - Limited

A Limited Durable Power of Attorney grants someone the authority to handle specific financial or legal matters on behalf of the principal while ensuring that only designated tasks can be managed. Unlike a general durable power of attorney, this document restricts the agent's authority to predefined actions rather than granting broad control over all affairs.

Why Use a Limited Durable Power of Attorney?

This document provides key advantages for situations where selective delegation is necessary:

- **Defines Scope Clearly:** Limits authority to specific tasks, such as handling a single real estate transaction or managing a particular account.
- **Maintains Control:** Ensures the principal retains full autonomy over areas not covered in the document.
- **Supports Temporary Needs:** Useful for situations like travel or medical incapacity when an agent is required for limited responsibilities.
- **Prevents Overreach:** Reduces risks associated with granting full financial control to another individual.

When Should You Use a Limited Durable Power of Attorney?

This document is beneficial when:

- **A business transaction** requires someone to act on your behalf.
- **Specific legal filings** need to be completed during a period of incapacity.
- **Temporary financial management** is needed while traveling or recovering from illness.

- **Handling single-purpose matters**, such as tax filings or banking actions.

How to Set Up and Use a Limited Durable Power of Attorney?

1. **Define the Scope of Authority:**
    - Specify exact tasks the agent can perform, ensuring limitations are clear.
2. **Select a Trusted Agent:**
    - Choose someone capable and reliable for the designated responsibilities.
3. **Draft the Legal Document:**
    - Work with an attorney to outline permissions and restrictions, ensuring clarity and enforceability.
4. **Sign and Notarize the Form:**
    - Follow state requirements for legal recognition, including necessary witness signatures.
5. **Distribute Copies to Relevant Parties:**
    - Provide copies to financial institutions, legal representatives, or other involved parties.
6. **Review and Adjust as Needed:**
    - Update the document if circumstances change or additional authority is required.

A Limited Durable Power of Attorney offers a controlled way to delegate specific tasks without granting unrestricted access to financial or legal affairs. Proper execution ensures security while allowing essential matters to be managed efficiently.

Durable Power of Attorney Limited

This DURABLE POWER OF ATTORNEY is made this _______ (Date), by and between:

Principal:

- Full Legal Name: ______________________________
- Address: ______________________________
- Phone Number: ______________________________
- Email Address (optional): ______________________________

Agent (Attorney-in-Fact):

- Full Legal Name: ______________________________
- Address: ______________________________
- Phone Number: ______________________________
- Email Address (optional): ______________________________

1. Designation of Agent

I, ______________________ (Full Name of Principal), hereby designate ______________________ (Full Name of Agent) as my Attorney-in-Fact to act for me in the following matters:

2. Specific Powers of Agent

My Agent is authorized to act only in the following specific matters:

- ____
- ____

- ______________________________
- ______________________________
- ______________________________

3. Duration of Power of Attorney

This Durable Power of Attorney shall become effective immediately upon signing and shall remain in effect until ________ (Date of Expiry) or until I revoke it in writing. This will allow the Agent to act on my behalf for the duration of the period specified above.

4. Revocation of Previous Powers of Attorney

This document revokes all prior Durable Powers of Attorney executed by me for the same purposes as outlined above, effective as of the signing of this document. However, this revocation will not affect any actions taken by my Agent prior to the revocation.

5. Agent's Duties and Responsibilities

My Agent agrees to act in good faith, with due care and diligence, and in accordance with the instructions I've provided in this Durable Power of Attorney. The Agent must maintain accurate records of all actions taken on my behalf and provide them to me upon request.

6. Liability of Agent

My Agent shall not be liable for any good faith actions taken within the scope of this Durable Power of Attorney. However, the Agent will be liable for actions that are grossly negligent, fraudulent, or beyond the authority granted by this document.

7. Successor Agent

If the designated Agent is unable or unwilling to serve, I appoint ____________________ (Full Name of Successor Agent) as the successor Agent, who will assume the same powers and responsibilities outlined above.

8. Revocation of Power of Attorney

I retain the right to revoke this Durable Power of Attorney at any time during my lifetime by providing written notice to my Agent and to any third parties relying on this document. The revocation will take effect upon delivery of such notice.

9. Signature and Acknowledgment

By signing this Durable Power of Attorney, I affirm that I am of sound mind and understand the powers I am granting to my Agent. I execute this document voluntarily, without duress, and with full understanding of its implications.

Principal's Signature: ____________________

Date: ____________________

Agent's Signature (acknowledging receipt of authority):

Agent's Signature: ____________________

Date: ____________________

10. Witnesses

This document must be signed in the presence of two (2) witnesses, who will verify the principal's identity and mental competency. The witnesses cannot be named as beneficiaries in the Durable Power of Attorney or have any financial interest in the principal's estate.

Witness 1's Signature: ____________________________

Date: ____________________________

Witness 2's Signature: ____________________________

Date: ____________________________

11. Notary Public (if applicable)

State of ____________________________

County of ____________________________

Subscribed and sworn before me on [Date], by ____________________ (Principal's Full Name), known to me or provided identification.

Notary's Signature: ____________________________

Date: ____________________________

Durable Power of Attorney for Healthcare

A Durable Power of Attorney for Healthcare is a legal document that designates a trusted individual (healthcare agent) to make medical decisions on behalf of the principal if they become incapacitated. This ensures that medical choices align with the individual's preferences even when they cannot communicate their wishes.

Why Use a Durable Power of Attorney for Healthcare?

This document provides several key benefits:

- **Ensures Medical Preferences Are Respected:** Allows someone to advocate for treatments based on the principal's values.
- **Avoids Delays in Medical Care:** Prevents treatment disruptions by eliminating the need for court-appointed guardianship.
- **Supports Loved Ones in Decision-Making:** Gives family members clarity and authority to make necessary healthcare choices.
- **Works Alongside an Advance Healthcare Directive:** Complements a living will by allowing an agent to make flexible medical decisions when needed.

When Should You Establish a Durable Power of Attorney for Healthcare?

It is best to create this document before a medical emergency occurs, especially in the following situations:

- **Aging individuals** planning for potential health-related incapacity.
- **People with chronic or life-threatening conditions** requiring ongoing medical management.

- **Anyone undergoing major surgery or treatment** with possible complications.
- Individuals who want to ensure their medical decisions are handled by someone they trust.

How to Set Up and Use a Durable Power of Attorney for Healthcare

1. **Choose a Healthcare Agent:**
   - Select a trustworthy individual familiar with your medical values and preferences.
   - Ensure they are willing and capable of making important healthcare decisions.
2. **Define the Scope of Authority:**
   - Specify whether the agent can decide on treatments, surgeries, medications, or end-of-life care.
   - Include any restrictions or personal requests regarding medical interventions.
3. **Draft the Legal Document:**
   - Work with an estate planning attorney or use state-approved forms to establish the power of attorney.
4. **Sign and Validate the Document:**
   - Follow state-specific legal requirements, including notarization or witness signatures.
5. **Distribute Copies to Healthcare Providers and Family:**
   - Ensure hospitals, doctors, and key family members have access to the doc-

ument.

6. **Review and Update as Needed:**

    ◦ Modify the document as health conditions or personal preferences change.

A Durable Power of Attorney for Healthcare guarantees that medical decisions align with an individual's wishes while ensuring seamless healthcare management during incapacitation. Proper planning prevents uncertainty and provides peace of mind for both the individual and their loved ones.

Durable Power of Attorney for Healthcare

I, ____________________ [Full Name of Principal], being of sound mind, voluntarily make this Living Will (Healthcare Directive) on this ________ (Date), to express my wishes regarding medical treatment in the event that I am unable to communicate or make decisions for myself due to a terminal illness, injury, or incapacity.

1. Declaration of Intent

In the event that I am diagnosed with a terminal condition, or if I am in a persistent vegetative state or coma, and there is no reasonable hope of recovery, I make the following decisions regarding my health care, including life-sustaining treatments and end-of-life care.

2. Appointment of Healthcare Agent

If I am unable to make decisions regarding my medical care, I appoint the following individual as my healthcare agent to make decisions on my behalf:

- **Healthcare Agent's Full Name:** ________________________________
- **Address:** ____
- **Phone Number**: ____

If my first choice is unable or unwilling to serve, I appoint the following individual as my alternate healthcare agent:

- **Alternate Healthcare Agent's Full Name** ________________________________
- **Address:** ____
- **Phone Number**: ____

3. General Powers of Healthcare Agent

My healthcare agent shall have the authority to make decisions about my medical care, including, but not limited to, the following:

- Consent to or refuse medical treatments, including surgeries, medications, and therapies;
- Decide whether to start, continue, or discontinue life-sustaining treatments;
- Choose healthcare providers and facilities;
- Access my medical records and share my health information with healthcare providers;
- Make decisions regarding organ donation and posthumous care.

4. End-of-Life Care Decisions

If I am diagnosed with a terminal condition or am in a persistent vegetative state with no reasonable chance of recovery, I request the following:

- **Life-Sustaining Treatments**: I do not wish to receive life-sustaining treatments (such as mechanical ventilation, CPR, dialysis, or feeding tubes) if my condition is terminal and recovery is not possible. I request that these treatments be withheld or discontinued, allowing me to pass naturally.
- **Artificial Nutrition and Hydration**: If I am in a terminal state and there is no reasonable hope of recovery, I do not wish to receive artificial nutrition or hydration through tubes or other medical devices. I prefer comfort care to alleviate my suffering.
- **Palliative Care**: I request that palliative care be provided to relieve my pain and suffering, even if such care may hasten my death. I wish to be made as comfortable as possible.

5. Specific Treatment Instructions

If I am in a situation where I am unable to make decisions for myself but I am not terminally ill or in a persistent vegetative state, I request the following medical treatments:

- **Pain Management**: I request the use of pain relief medications, including narcotics, as necessary to alleviate my suffering, even if such treatment may hasten my death.
- **Blood Transfusions**: I do not wish to receive blood transfusions under any circumstances.
- **Antibiotics and Other Treatments**: I request that all reasonable efforts be made to prevent infections and to treat my illness unless it is clear that such treatments would only prolong my suffering.

6. Organ Donation

Upon my death, I wish to donate my organs and tissues for transplantation or medical research, if suitable for donation. I consent to the following:

- **Organ Donation**: I consent to the donation of my organs, including but not limited to my heart, kidneys, liver, and lungs.
- **Tissue Donation**: I consent to the donation of my tissues for medical research or educational purposes.

If I do not wish to donate my organs or tissues, I direct that no donation be made.

7. Pregnancy and Reproductive Health (if applicable)

If I am pregnant and in a situation where I am unable to make medical decisions for myself, I request the following:

- **Life-Saving Treatment**: If my life is at risk due to my pregnancy, I request that lifesaving treatments be provided, even if it results in the termination of the pregnancy.
- **Non-Viable Pregnancy**: If the pregnancy is non-viable or the fetus has a fatal condition, I request that no efforts be made to prolong the pregnancy.

8. Nomination of Guardian for Minor Children (if applicable)

In the event that I am incapacitated and unable to care for my minor children, I nominate the following individual as the guardian of my minor children:

- **Guardian's Full Name:** ___________________________________
- **Address:** ____
- **Phone Number**: _______________________________________

9. Revocation of Prior Directives

I hereby revoke any prior health care directives, living wills, or powers of attorney for healthcare that I have previously executed. This Living Will shall serve as my most current and binding directive regarding my health care wishes.

10. Statement of Intent

I affirm that I am of sound mind and have executed this Living Will (Healthcare Directive) voluntarily. I understand that it will guide my health care decisions and those of my healthcare agent if I become incapacitated.

11. Signature of Principal

I, ________________________ [Principal's Full Name], being of sound mind, voluntarily execute this Living Will on this _______ (Date).

Principal's Signature: ____________________________

Date: ____________________________

12. Witnesses

This document was executed by [Principal's Full Name] in the presence of the undersigned witnesses, who affirm that the Principal is of sound mind and voluntarily signing this document.

Witness 1's Signature: ___________________________

Date: ___________________________

Witness 2's Signature: ___________________________

Date: ___________________________

13. Notary Public (if required)

State of _______ [State]

County of ________ [County]

On this _______ [Date], before me, a Notary Public, personally appeared __________________ [Principal's Full Name], known to me or provided identification, and acknowledged that they executed the same for the purposes therein contained.

Notary's Signature: ___________________________

Date: ___________________________

Advance Healthcare Directive Living Will

An Advance Healthcare Directive, commonly known as a Living Will, is a legal document that outlines an individual's medical treatment preferences and end-of-life care instructions in case they become seriously ill or incapacitated. It ensures that healthcare providers and loved ones follow the individual's wishes regarding medical interventions and life-sustaining treatments.

Why Use an Advance Healthcare Directive?

This document provides several essential benefits:

- **Clarifies Treatment Preferences:** Ensures medical decisions align with the individual's values and wishes.
- **Prevents Family Uncertainty:** Reduces emotional stress for loved ones by eliminating guesswork in critical situations.
- **Guides Healthcare Providers:** Helps doctors make informed decisions based on the patient's pre-stated instructions.
- **Avoids Unwanted Medical Interventions:** Ensures that unnecessary or undesired treatments are not administered.

When Should You Create an Advance Healthcare Directive?

It is best to establish a Living Will before any medical emergency arises, particularly in the following cases:

- **Aging individuals** who want to ensure control over their healthcare choices.
- **People with chronic or life-threatening illnesses** who anticipate potential medical complications.
- **Those undergoing high-risk medical procedures** where advance planning

may be necessary.

- **Anyone who wants peace of mind** knowing their healthcare preferences will be respected.

How to Set Up and Use an Advance Healthcare Directive

1. **Define Medical Preferences:**
    - Specify which treatments you want or do not want, including life support, resuscitation, tube feeding, and pain management.
2. **Appoint a Healthcare Proxy:**
    - Choose a trusted individual to make medical decisions on your behalf if needed.
    - Ensure they understand and agree to uphold your wishes.
3. **Draft and Legally Validate the Document:**
    - Work with an attorney or use state-approved forms to create a legally binding directive.
    - Ensure the document complies with local laws and healthcare regulations.
4. **Share Copies with Healthcare Providers and Family:**
    - Provide copies to doctors, hospitals, and key family members so they are aware of your preferences.
5. **Review and Update Periodically:**
    - Revise the directive to reflect changes in medical conditions or personal preferences.

An Advance Healthcare Directive ensures that medical decisions align with an individual's values while providing peace of mind to loved ones during difficult situations.

Keeping it updated and accessible allows for smooth healthcare decision-making when needed.

Advanced Health Care Directive Living Will

I, ______________________________ [Full Name of Principal], being of sound mind, voluntarily make this Advanced Health Care Directive (Living Will) on this _______ (Date), to express my wishes regarding medical treatment in the event that I become unable to communicate or make decisions for myself due to an illness, injury, or incapacity.

1. Declaration of Intent

In the event that I am diagnosed with a terminal condition or am in a persistent vegetative state or coma, and there is no reasonable hope of recovery, I make the following health care decisions regarding life-sustaining treatments and end-of-life care.

2. Appointment of Health Care Agent

If I am unable to make decisions regarding my medical care, I appoint the following individual as my Health Care Agent to make medical decisions on my behalf:

- **Health Care Agent's Full Name:** ______________________________
- **Address:** ______________________________
- **Phone Number:** ______________________________

If my first choice is unable or unwilling to serve, I appoint the following individual as my alternate Health Care Agent:

- **Alternate Health Care Agent's Full Name:** ______________________________
- **Address:** ______________________________
- **Phone Number:** ______________________________

3. General Powers of Health Care Agent

My Health Care Agent is authorized to make decisions about my medical treatment, including, but not limited to, the following:

- Deciding whether to start, stop, or continue life-sustaining treatments;
- Consenting to or refusing medical procedures, including surgery, medications, and treatments;
- Choosing health care providers and facilities;
- Accessing my medical records and sharing my health information with others involved in my care;
- Making decisions about organ donation and posthumous care.

4. End-of-Life Care Decisions

If I am diagnosed with a terminal condition or am in a persistent vegetative state with no reasonable chance of recovery, I request the following:

- **Life-Sustaining Treatments:** I do not want life-sustaining treatments (such as mechanical ventilation, dialysis, or CPR) if my condition is terminal and recovery is not possible. I request that these treatments be withheld or discontinued, allowing me to pass naturally.
- **Artificial Nutrition and Hydration**: I do not want to be artificially fed or hydrated (through tubes or other devices) if I am in a terminal state and there is no reasonable chance of recovery.
- **Palliative Care**: I request that I be given palliative care to alleviate pain and suffering, even if it may hasten my death. I wish to be made as comfortable as possible.

5. Specific Treatment Instructions

If I am in a situation where I can no longer make decisions for myself but I am not terminally ill or in a persistent vegetative state, I request the following medical treatments:

[List any specific medical treatments or procedures the principal would like to request or refuse.]

- Example: **Pain management**: I request pain management, including the use of narcotics if necessary to alleviate my suffering.
- Example: **Blood Transfusions**: I refuse blood transfusions under any circumstance.

6. Organ Donation

Upon my death, I wish to donate my organs and tissues for transplantation or medical research, if deemed medically suitable. I request the following:

- **Organ Donation**: I consent to the donation of my organs, including my heart, kidneys, liver, lungs, and other tissues.
- **Donation of Body for Medical Research**: I consent to the donation of my body for medical research or educational purposes.

If I do not wish to donate organs or tissues, I direct that no donation be made.

7. Pregnancy and Reproductive Health (if applicable)

If I am pregnant and in a situation where I am unable to make medical decisions for myself, I request the following:

- **Life-Saving Treatment**: If my life is at risk due to my pregnancy, I request that lifesaving treatment be provided, even if it results in the termination of the pregnancy.
- **Non-Viable Pregnancy**: If the pregnancy is non-viable or the fetus has a fatal condition, I request that no efforts be made to prolong the pregnancy.

8. Nomination of Guardian for Minor Children (if applicable)

In the event that I am incapacitated and unable to care for my minor children, I nominate the following individual as their guardian:

- Guardian's Full Name: ________________________
- Address: ________________________
- Phone Number: ________________________

9. Revocation of Prior Directives

This Advanced Health Care Directive revokes any prior directives regarding my medical care, including any previous living wills or health care powers of attorney, and shall serve as my sole directive regarding my health care wishes.

10. Statement of Intent

I affirm that I am of sound mind and have executed this document voluntarily. I understand that this directive will guide my health care decisions and those of my Health Care Agent if I become incapacitated.

11. Signature of Principal

I, ________________________ [Principal's Full Name], being of sound mind, voluntarily execute this Advanced Health Care Directive (Living Will) on this _______ (Date). By signing, I acknowledge that I understand its contents and the authority granted to my Health Care Agent.

Principal's Signature: ________________________

Date: ________________________

12. Witnesses

This document was executed by [Principal's Full Name] in the presence of the undersigned witnesses, who affirm that the Principal is of sound mind and is voluntarily signing this document.

Witness 1's Signature: ___________________________

Date: ___________________________

Witness 2's Signature: ___________________________

Date: ___________________________

13. Notary Public (if required)

State of [State]

County of [County]

On this ____________ [Date], before me, a Notary Public, personally appeared ________________ [Principal's Full Name], known to me or provided identification, and acknowledged that they executed the same for the purposes therein contained.

Notary's Signature: ___________________________

Date: ___________________________

HIPAA Authorization Form

A HIPAA Authorization Form allows an individual to designate specific people who can access their protected health information (PHI) under the Health Insurance Portability and Accountability Act (HIPAA). This document ensures healthcare providers can share medical updates with chosen family members or representatives.

Why Use a HIPAA Authorization Form?

This form provides several crucial benefits:

- **Ensures Loved Ones Can Access Medical Information:** Without written authorization, even close family members may be restricted from receiving updates.

- **Supports Healthcare Decision-Making:** Helps designated individuals stay informed when making medical choices on the patient's behalf.

- **Avoids Legal Barriers:** Prevents delays in treatment or coordination due to privacy regulations.

- **Provides Flexibility:** Allows you to specify exactly who can access medical details and what information they can receive.

When Should You Complete a HIPAA Authorization Form?

This document should be established **before a medical emergency occurs** to prevent complications. Common situations where it is useful include:

- **Planned surgeries or major medical treatments** requiring ongoing updates.

- **Managing healthcare for aging individuals** who need family involvement in medical decisions.

- **Ensuring access for spouses, adult children, or caregivers** to critical health records.

- **Allowing legal representatives** to handle healthcare coordination when necessary.

How to Set Up and Use a HIPAA Authorization Form?

1. **Identify Authorized Individuals:**
   - List trusted family members, caregivers, or legal representatives.
   - Specify whether access is full or limited to specific types of health information.
2. **Complete the Authorization Form:**
   - Use the provider's official form or a legally recognized template.
   - Clearly outline the scope of medical information that can be shared.
3. **Sign and Submit the Form:**
   - Ensure proper signatures and compliance with legal requirements.
   - Submit the document to healthcare providers or institutions.
4. **Distribute Copies to Relevant Parties:**
   - Provide copies to authorized individuals and medical professionals.
5. **Review and Update Periodically:**
   - Adjust authorization as medical needs or family circumstances change.

A HIPAA Authorization Form ensures that trusted individuals can access vital medical information while maintaining healthcare privacy protections. Keeping it up to date allows for smooth communication and better-informed medical decisions when needed.

HIPAA AUTHORIZATION FORM

I, ______________________ [Full Name of Patient], hereby authorize the use and disclosure of my protected health information (PHI) under the Health Insurance Portability and Accountability Act (HIPAA) for the purposes stated in this authorization. This authorization allows the release of my health information to the designated recipient(s) listed below.

1. Patient Information

- Full Legal Name: ______________________________________
- Date of Birth: ______________________________________
- Address: ______________________________________
- Phone Number: ______________________________________
- Email Address (optional): ______________________________

2. Person/Organization Authorized to Disclose Health Information

I authorize the following person(s) or organization(s) to disclose my protected health information (PHI):

- Name of Entity: ______________________________________
- Address: ______________________________________
- Phone Number: ______________________________________
- Email Address (optional): ______________________________

3. Person/Organization Receiving Health Information

I authorize the following person(s) or organization(s) to receive my protected health information:

- Name: ______________________________________
- Address: ______________________________________

- Phone Number: ______________________________
- Email Address (optional): ________________________

4. Purpose of Disclosure

The purpose for which my health information is being disclosed is:

[ ] Continuing medical care and treatment

[ ] Insurance purposes

[ ] Legal purposes

[ ] Employment-related reasons

[ ] Personal request

[ ] Other: ____

5. Description of Health Information to be Disclosed

The following types of health information will be disclosed under this authorization:

- Medical history (includes diagnoses, conditions, treatments, etc.)
- Mental health information (if applicable, include therapy, medications, etc.)
- Test results (lab reports, imaging, etc.)
- Treatment records (including physician notes, hospital records)
- Other: __________________________________

6. Expiration of Authorization

This authorization will expire on the following date, event, or condition:

[ ] One year from the date of signing

[ ] Specific date: ______________________________

[ ] Upon completion of the purpose of disclosure

[ ] No expiration date (if applicable)

7. Right to Revoke Authorization

I understand that I have the right to revoke this authorization at any time by submitting a written revocation to the entity to which I granted this authorization. My revocation will not affect any disclosures made prior to the date the revocation is received.

8. Potential for Re-disclosure

I understand that once my health information is disclosed to the recipient(s) listed above, it may no longer be protected under HIPAA and may be subject to re-disclosure. I understand that the recipient(s) of my health information may further disclose it, but they are not required to do so.

9. Signature and Acknowledgment

I understand that by signing this form, I am authorizing the disclosure of my health information as outlined above. I affirm that I am the patient, or the authorized representative of the patient, and that I have the legal right to authorize the disclosure of this health information.

Patient's Signature: ______________________________

Date: ______________________________

Authorized Representative's Signature (if applicable):

- Full Name: ______________________________

- Relationship to Patient: ______________________
- Date: ______________________

10. Witness (Optional)

This document was signed in the presence of the undersigned witness, who affirms that the patient (or authorized representative) signed this form voluntarily and understands the purpose and implications of this authorization.

Witness 1's Signature: ______________________

Date: ______________________

11. Notary Public (Optional, if required)

State of [State]

County of [County]

Subscribed and sworn before me on this [Date], by [Patient's Full Name], known to me to be the person whose name is subscribed to this instrument and acknowledged that they executed the same for the purposes therein contained.

Notary's Signature: ______________________

Date: ______________________

Certification of Trust

A Certification of Trust is a legal document that provides proof of a trust's existence without disclosing sensitive details. It contains essential information required for financial and legal transactions while safeguarding the privacy of the trust's terms and beneficiaries.

Why Use a Certification of Trust?

This document offers several key advantages:

- **Verifies the Trust's Legality:** Confirms the trust exists and is properly established.
- **Maintains Privacy:** Prevents disclosure of personal details, such as beneficiaries and specific asset distributions.
- **Speeds Up Transactions:** Allows financial institutions, insurance providers, and real estate entities to process requests without requiring a full trust document.
- **Simplifies Administrative Procedures:** Reduces unnecessary paperwork by offering a concise overview of the trust.

When Should You Use a Certification of Trust?

A Certification of Trust is typically required when:

- **Opening or managing bank accounts** under the trust's name.
- **Handling insurance policies** that involve trust assets.
- **Executing real estate transactions** where property is held in a trust.
- **Interacting with financial institutions** that require proof of trust ownership.

How to Prepare a Certification of Trust?

1. **Include Essential Information:**
    - Trust's legal name and establishment date.
    - The trustee's name and authority.
    - Confirmation that the trust is legally valid.
2. **Exclude Confidential Details:**
    - Avoid listing beneficiaries, asset values, or specific terms of the trust.
3. **Ensure Legal Compliance:**
    - Work with an estate planning attorney to meet state-specific requirements.
4. **Sign and Notarize the Document:**
    - Some institutions may require notarization for validation.
5. **Provide Copies When Necessary:**
    - Share the certification with banks, insurers, or real estate professionals upon request.

A Certification of Trust offers a streamlined and confidential way to prove a trust's existence while ensuring efficiency in financial and legal transactions. Keeping it readily available helps facilitate estate management and protects personal details.

Certification of Trust

This CERTIFICATION OF TRUST is made on this ________ [Date], by and between:

Trustee:

- Full Legal Name: ______________________________
- Address: ______________________________
- Phone Number: ______________________________
- Email Address (optional): ______________________________

Trust Name:

- Name of Trust: ______________________________
- Date of Trust Agreement: ______________________________

1. Declaration of Trust

I, ______________ [Trustee's Full Name], as Trustee of the __________ [Trust Name] Revocable Living Trust, hereby certify that the Trust Agreement referenced above is in full effect, and that I am the currently acting Trustee of this Trust.

2. Powers of the Trustee

I affirm that I have full authority to manage, transfer, and distribute assets held in the ____________________ [Trust Name] Revocable Living Trust. The powers granted to me include, but are not limited to, managing real estate, financial accounts, and investments, and executing any documents related to these assets in accordance with the terms of the Trust Agreement.

3. Identification of Trust

- **Date the Trust was Created**: ______________________
- **Trust's Purpose**: [Purpose of the Trust, e.g., "To manage assets for the benefit of the

Beneficiaries and ensure a smooth transfer of assets upon the Grantor's death."]

4. Trust Details

Trustee(s):

- Primary Trustee: [Trustee's Full Name]
- Successor Trustee(s) (if applicable): [Successor Trustee's Full Name]

Beneficiaries: The primary beneficiaries of the Trust are as follows:

- [Beneficiary 1's Full Name]
- [Beneficiary 2's Full Name]
- [Beneficiary 3's Full Name]

Successor Trustee(s): In the event the current Trustee is unable to serve, I appoint ______________________ [Successor Trustee's Full Name] as the Successor Trustee, who shall manage the Trust assets in accordance with the terms of the Trust Agreement.

5. Acknowledgment of Trust Provisions

I acknowledge that the following provisions are part of the ______________ [Trust Name] Revocable Living Trust:

- **Revocability**: This Trust is revocable during my lifetime, and the Grantor retains the right to amend or revoke the Trust.
- **Assets in Trust**: The assets held within the Trust include real estate, bank accounts, investment accounts, and personal property.

- **Distribution Upon Death:** Upon the death of the Grantor, the Trustee shall distribute the assets of the Trust to the designated beneficiaries as provided in the Trust Agreement.

6. Certification of No Change to Trust

This Certification of Trust accurately reflects the terms of the Trust and certifies that there have been no changes to the Trust Agreement since its creation on ______________ [Date of Trust Agreement]. If there have been any amendments to the Trust, such amendments are attached to this document.

7. Trustee's Authority to Act

This Certification of Trust grants the undersigned Trustee the authority to manage the Trust's assets, including but not limited to:

- Selling, transferring, or mortgaging real property;
- Managing and making decisions regarding investments and financial accounts;
- Handling tax-related matters concerning the Trust's assets;
- Distributing Trust assets to the beneficiaries as instructed by the terms of the Trust.

8. Trustee's Indemnification

The Trustee shall be indemnified from any liability, claims, or expenses incurred in the administration of the Trust, as long as the Trustee acts in good faith and in accordance with the Trust's terms and applicable law.

9.Trust Duration and Termination

This Trust shall remain in effect during the Grantor's lifetime unless revoked or amended by the Grantor. Upon the Grantor's death, the Trust will continue to exist for the benefit of the beneficiaries, and the Trustee shall manage the Trust assets until they are distributed according to the Trust's terms. The Trust will terminate upon the full distribution of its assets.

10. Signature of Trustee

I, ____________________________ [Trustee's Full Name], as Trustee of the ____________________ [Trust Name] Revocable Living Trust, certify under penalty of perjury that the above information is accurate and reflects the terms of the Trust Agreement.

Trustee's Signature: ______________________________

Date: ______________________________

11. Witnesses (if required)

We, the undersigned witnesses, hereby affirm that ____________________________ [Trustee's Full Name], the Trustee, executed this Certification of Trust in our presence, and to the best of our knowledge, the Trustee is acting in accordance with the terms of the Trust.

Witness 1's Signature: ______________________________

Date: ______________________________

Witness 2's Signature: ______________________________

Date: ______________________________

12. Notary Public (if required)

State of ___________ [State]

County of _____________ [County]

On this_______ [Date], before me, a Notary Public, personally appeared _---- _________________ [Trustee's Full Name], known to me to be the person whose name is subscribed to this instrument and acknowledged that they executed the same for the purposes therein contained.

Notary's Signature: ___________________________

Date: ___________________________

Guardian Designation for Minor Children

A Guardian Designation is a legal document that determines who will care for a child if both parents pass away before the child reaches adulthood. It ensures that the child is raised by someone chosen by the parents rather than leaving the decision to a court.

Why Use a Guardian Designation?

This document offers several key benefits:

- **Ensures Parental Wishes Are Respected:** Allows parents to select trusted guardians rather than leaving the decision to legal proceedings.
- **Avoids Lengthy Court Battles:** Prevents disputes over custody that could delay a child's care.
- **Provides Stability and Security:** Ensures children are placed in a home that aligns with parental values.
- **Addresses Emergency Situations:** Allows for a clear transition in case of unforeseen circumstances.

When Should You Establish a Guardian Designation?

Parents should create a Guardian Designation as soon as they have young children to ensure protection. Specific instances when it is especially important include:

- **Single parents** who want to establish clear caregiving plans.
- **Parents traveling frequently** or working in high-risk professions.
- **Families with specific personal or religious preferences** for child-rearing.
- **Parents with health concerns** that may impact their ability to provide long-term care.

How to Set Up and Use a Guardian Designation?

1. **Select a Suitable Guardian:**
    - Choose someone who shares similar values and parenting philosophies.
    - Ensure they are financially and emotionally prepared to take on responsibility.
2. **Draft a Legal Document:**
    - Work with an attorney or use state-approved forms to formalize the designation.
    - Include alternate guardians in case the primary choice is unable to serve.
3. **Sign and Notarize the Document:**
    - Ensure all legal formalities are completed to validate the designation.
4. **Communicate With the Guardian:**
    - Discuss expectations and responsibilities to ensure alignment with parental wishes.
5. **Review and Update Periodically:**
    - Modify the designation as circumstances change, such as new guardian availability or evolving family needs.

A Guardian Designation provides peace of mind by ensuring a child's future care is properly planned. Establishing this document early prevents uncertainty and guarantees that children receive support in a stable, loving environment.

Guardianship Designation for Minor Children

This GUARDIANSHIP DESIGNATION is made this ________ (Date), by and between:

Parent/Legal Guardian:

- Full Legal Name: ____
- Address: ____
- Phone Number: ____
- Email Address (optional): _______________________________

Minor Children:

- Child 1: ________________ [Full Name], Date of Birth: ______________________
- Child 2: ____________________ [Full Name], Date of Birth: ______________________
- [List any additional children as necessary]

1. Appointment of Primary Guardian

In the event of my death or incapacity, I hereby designate the following individual as the primary guardian of my minor children:

- Guardian's Full Name: _______________________________
- Address: ____________________________________
- Phone Number: ________________________________

This guardian shall be responsible for providing care, education, and general welfare to my children, including making all necessary decisions related to their upbringing, medical care, and schooling.

2. Appointment of Alternate Guardian

If the primary guardian is unable or unwilling to serve as guardian of my minor children, I designate the following individual as the alternate guardian:

- Alternate Guardian's Full Name: ____________________
- Address: ____________________
- Phone Number: ____________________

This alternate guardian shall assume responsibility for the care of my minor children upon the death or incapacity of the primary guardian.

3. Instructions for Guardianship

In the event of my death or incapacity, I request that the appointed guardian provide the following for my children:

- **Medical Care:** I wish for my children to receive all necessary medical treatment and healthcare as required by their needs.
- **Educational Needs:** I wish for my children to receive education in accordance with their abilities and potential, including choosing suitable schools and extracurricular activities.
- **Religious/Spiritual Needs:** [If applicable, specify the desired religious or spiritual upbringing for the children.]

4. Financial Support for the Children

I direct that the financial assets in my estate or Trust be used for the care, support, and maintenance of my minor children, including but not limited to:

- Food, shelter, clothing, and medical expenses
- Educational expenses, including tuition, books, and related costs
- Extracurricular activities or specialized care as needed

I trust the appointed guardian to manage these funds responsibly and in the best interests of my children.

5. Special Instructions for the Children's Care

If there are any special needs or considerations for my children, I provide the following instructions for their care:

- [Specify any medical conditions, disabilities, or special needs the children may have, and the required care.]
- [If applicable, specify the children's routine, lifestyle preferences, or other unique instructions.]

6. Revocation of Previous Guardianship Designations

This document revokes any prior guardianship designations made by me regarding the care of my minor children, and this document shall serve as the only valid designation for guardianship.

7. Acknowledgment of Guardianship Designation

I affirm that I am of sound mind and voluntarily execute this Guardianship Designation for Minor Children. I understand that it will guide the appointed guardian(s) in caring for my children in the event of my death or incapacity.

8. Signature of Parent/Legal Guardian

I, ______________________ [Parent's Full Name], being of sound mind, voluntarily execute this Guardianship Designation for Minor Children on this _______ (Date).

Parent/Legal Guardian's Signature: ___________________________

Date: ___________________________

9. Witnesses

This document must be signed in the presence of two (2) witnesses who are not named as guardians in this document and who affirm that the parent/legal guardian is of sound mind and is signing the document voluntarily.

Witness 1's Signature: ____________________________

Date: ____________________________

Witness 2's Signature: ____________________________

Date: ____________________________

10. Notary Public (if required)

State of [State]

County of [County]

On this ____________ [Date], before me, a Notary Public, personally appeared ____________________ [Parent's Full Name], known to me or provided identification, and acknowledged that they executed the same for the purposes therein contained.

Notary's Signature: ____________________________

Date: ____________________________

Pet Trust

A Pet Trust is a legal arrangement that ensures a pet's financial and caregiving needs are met if the owner passes away or becomes unable to care for them. It allows pet owners to set aside funds and specify care instructions to guarantee their animal's well-being.

Why Use a Pet Trust?

Creating a Pet Trust offers several important benefits:

- **Provides Financial Security:** Ensures money is available for food, medical care, and other pet-related expenses.
- **Prevents Uncertainty:** Establishes clear instructions, preventing pets from being abandoned or placed in shelters.
- **Designates a Caregiver:** Names a trusted individual or organization responsible for looking after the pet.
- **Avoids Legal Complications:** Protects against disputes regarding pet ownership after the owner's passing.

When Should You Set Up a Pet Trust?

A Pet Trust should be established **as soon as you have a pet**, particularly in the following situations:

- **Owning pets with long lifespans**, such as birds, turtles, or certain breeds of dogs and cats.
- **Having specific care requirements**, like medications or specialized diets.
- **Living alone or without close family members who would naturally care for the pet.**

- Wanting to ensure your pet's well-being and quality of life in any unforeseen circumstance.

Wanting to ensure your pet's well-being and quality of life in any unforeseen circumstance.

How to Set Up and Use a Pet Trust?

1. **Choose a Caregiver (Trustee):**
   - Select a reliable person or organization to care for the pet.
   - Ensure they are willing and able to take on the responsibility.
2. **Set Aside Funds for Pet Care:**
   - Estimate costs for food, veterinary expenses, grooming, and other necessities.
   - Allocate a reasonable amount that covers lifelong care.
3. **Define Care Instructions:**
   - Specify dietary needs, medical treatments, daily routines, and preferred living arrangements.
   - Include details such as exercise requirements and favorite activities.
4. **Draft a Legally Valid Pet Trust Document:**
   - Work with an attorney to ensure compliance with state laws.
   - Include clauses on fund management and pet transition in case the initial caregiver can no longer care for them.
5. **Review and Update as Needed:**
   - Modify the trust if a pet's needs change, such as medical conditions or new caregivers.

- Ensure funds remain sufficient over time.

A Pet Trust provides security and continuity for a beloved companion, ensuring their well-being even in unexpected circumstances. Proper planning prevents uncertainty and guarantees pets receive the care they deserve.

Pet Trust Clause

This PET TRUST AGREEMENT is made on this ________ (Date), by and between:

Grantor:

- Full Legal Name: ____
- Address: ____
- Phone Number: ____
- Email Address (optional): ______________________________

Trustee (the individual or institution managing the Trust):

- Full Legal Name: ____
- Address: ____
- Phone Number: ____
- Email Address (optional): ______________________________

Caregiver (the individual responsible for the day-to-day care of the pet):

- Full Legal Name: ____
- Address: ____
- Phone Number: ____
- Email Address (optional): ______________________________

Beneficiary (the pet(s) to be cared for under this Trust):

- Pet 1: Name: __________________________; Species: _______________; Breed: _____________; Date of Birth: ___________
- Pet 2: Name: __________________________; Species: _______________; Breed: _____________; Date of Birth: ___________
- [Add additional pets if applicable]

1. Purpose of the Trust

The purpose of this Pet Trust is to provide for the care, maintenance, and well-being of my pet(s), ________________ [Pet(s)' Full Name(s)], in the event of my death or incapacity. This Trust is designed to ensure that my pet(s) will receive continued care and protection throughout their lifetimes.

2. Appointment of Trustee

I hereby appoint ______________________ [Trustee's Full Name] as Trustee of this Pet Trust. If ____________________ [Trustee's Full Name] is unable or unwilling to serve, I appoint ____________________ [Alternate Trustee's Full Name] as Successor Trustee to serve in the Trustee's place. The Trustee shall be responsible for managing the assets of this Trust and ensuring that my pet(s) receive the care outlined in this document.

3. Appointment of Caregiver

I appoint ______________________ [Caregiver's Full Name] as the primary caregiver for my pet(s). The caregiver shall be responsible for the day-to-day care of my pet(s), including providing food, shelter, medical care, and other necessary services.

In the event that _____________________ [Caregiver's Full Name] is unable or unwilling to care for my pet(s), I appoint ________________________ [Alternate Caregiver's Full Name] as the successor caregiver.

4. Funding of the Trust

The Trust shall be funded with the sum of $[Amount] or other assets as designated by the Grantor, which shall be used solely for the care and well-being of my pet(s).

Initial Funding: The Trust shall be funded with the following assets:

- Cash: $______________________

- [Additional assets, such as insurance policies, real property, etc.]

The Trustee is authorized to use these funds in a manner that ensures the pet(s) receive proper care.

5. Trustee's Powers and Responsibilities

The Trustee is granted the following powers and responsibilities:

- To use the funds in the Trust to provide for the care and well-being of my pet(s).
- To make distributions from the Trust for necessary expenses such as food, medical care, grooming, and veterinary visits.
- To ensure that my pet(s) are housed in a safe and suitable environment, either with the designated caregiver or in a facility that meets my pet(s)' needs.
- To make reasonable decisions regarding the best interests of my pet(s), including decisions about medical treatment, surgery, and long-term care.

6. Care Instructions for Pet(s)

I request that the Trustee and caregiver follow the following instructions regarding the care of my pet(s):

- **Food and Nutrition**: My pet(s) should be provided with the following type of food:
  [Specify brand or type of food].
- **Veterinary Care:** I request that my pet(s) receive regular veterinary check-ups and necessary medical treatment.
- **Housing and Environment**: My pet(s) should be housed in a safe, clean, and secure environment, either with the designated caregiver or at a facility where they are comfortable.
- **Other Special Needs**: [Specify any special needs such as medications, mobility aids, behavior training, etc.]

7. Distributions from the Trust

The Trustee shall use the funds from the Trust to cover the following expenses for my pet(s):

- **Veterinary Expenses**: To cover routine medical care, vaccinations, emergency medical care, surgeries, and any other necessary treatments.
- **Food and Supplies**: To provide for the daily food, shelter, and other necessary supplies, including toys, bedding, and grooming.
- **Transportation**: To cover any transportation costs for my pet(s) to veterinary appointments or other required services.
- **Recreational and Social Activities**: To cover the costs of recreation and social activities to ensure my pet(s) lead a healthy, enriched life.

The Trustee is authorized to distribute the funds as needed to meet these needs, without disqualifying my pet(s) from any government assistance programs (if applicable).

8. Successor Trustee

If the Trustee is unable or unwilling to serve, the following individual(s) are appointed as Successor Trustee(s) in the following order:

1. ______________________________ [Successor Trustee 1's Full Name]

2. ______________________________ [Successor Trustee 2's Full Name] (if applicable)

The Successor Trustee shall assume all responsibilities and powers outlined in this Trust Agreement.

9. Termination of the Trust

The Trust shall terminate upon the death of the last surviving pet. Upon termination, any remaining assets in the Trust shall be distributed as follows:

- **Remaining Assets:** Any remaining assets in the Trust, after my pet(s) have passed away, shall be distributed to ____________________ [Beneficiary's Full Name] or to ______________________ [Charitable Organization Name], as specified by me in a separate document or by the terms of this Trust.

10. Trustee's Compensation

The Trustee may receive reasonable compensation for their services in managing the Trust. If the Trustee is a family member or close friend, they may serve without compensation unless otherwise specified in this document.

11. Miscellaneous Provisions

- **Spendthrift Clause:** The assets in the Trust are not subject to the claims of creditors of the Beneficiary or Trustee.
- **No Contest Clause:** If any beneficiary or interested party contests this Trust or challenges its terms, they shall forfeit any claim to the Trust's assets.

12. Governing Law

This Trust shall be governed by the laws of the State of [State], and any disputes regarding the administration of the Trust shall be subject to the jurisdiction of the courts in ____________ [County], ______________ [State].

13. Signature of Grantor (Settlor)

I, __________________ [Grantor's Full Name], being of sound mind, voluntarily execute this Pet Trust Agreement on this _______ (Date).

Grantor's Signature: ____________________________

Date: ____________________________

14. Signature of Trustee

I, ______________ [Trustee's Full Name], hereby accept the role of Trustee of the Pet Trust and agree to abide by the terms and conditions set forth in this Trust Agreement.

Trustee's Signature: ____________________________

Date: ____________________________

15. Witnesses (if required)

This document has been signed in the presence of the undersigned witnesses, who affirm that the Grantor is of sound mind and is signing this document voluntarily.

Witness 1's Signature: ____________________________

Date: ____________________________

Witness 2's Signature: ____________________________

Date: ____________________________

16. Notary Public (if required)

State of [State]

County of [County]

On this ___________ [Date], before me, a Notary Public, personally appeared _______________ [Testator's Full Name] and _____________ [Trustee's Full Name], known to me or provided identification, and acknowledged that they executed the same for the purposes therein contained.

Notary's Signature: ___________________________

Date: ___________________________

Beneficiary Designation Forms

Beneficiary Designation Forms are documents used to assign specific recipients for assets like retirement accounts, life insurance policies, and bank accounts after the owner's passing. Naming beneficiaries ensures these assets transfer directly to the intended recipients without going through probate.

Why Use Beneficiary Designation Forms?

This process provides several advantages:

- **Avoids Probate:** Assets pass directly to beneficiaries, bypassing court procedures.

- **Ensures Trust Compliance:** Ensures assets follow the trust's plan instead of defaulting to probate laws.

- **Speeds Up Asset Transfers:** Reduces delays in distributing funds, allowing beneficiaries quicker access.

- **Prevents Legal Disputes:** Clearly outlines who receives specific assets, minimizing conflicts among heirs.

When Should You Complete Beneficiary Designation Forms?

These forms should be **submitted after the trust is created** to align financial accounts with estate plans. They are especially necessary when:

- **Establishing or updating a trust** to ensure all assets follow its distribution plan.

- **Holding assets in retirement accounts or life insurance policies** that need designated beneficiaries.

- **Updating financial records** after major life changes such as marriage, divorce, or the birth of a child.

How to Set Up and Use Beneficiary Designation Forms?

1. **Identify Eligible Assets:**
   - Determine which accounts require a beneficiary designation, including retirement funds, insurance policies, and bank accounts.
2. **Select the Beneficiary:**
   - Assign individuals or a trust as the beneficiary.
   - Ensure names match legal documents to avoid discrepancies.
3. **Complete the Forms Through Financial Institutions:**
   - Request official forms from banks, investment firms, or insurance providers.
   - Fill out and submit them with the required details.
4. **Confirm Trust Alignment:**
   - Verify that designations match the trust's plan for asset distribution.
5. **Review and Update as Needed:**
   - Adjust beneficiaries when financial situations or family structures change.

Beneficiary Designation Forms ensure estate planning stays efficient, preventing probate complications and guaranteeing assets go to the right individuals or trust accounts. Keeping them updated and properly aligned secures a smooth transition after the owner's passing.

Beneficiary Designation Form

This BENEFICIARY DESIGNATION FORM is made on this _______ (Date), by and between:

Account Holder (Principal):

- Full Legal Name: ____________________
- Address: ____________________
- Phone Number: ____________________
- Email Address (optional): ____________________

1. Account Information

This Beneficiary Designation applies to the following account(s) owned by the undersigned:

- **Account Type:** [Life Insurance, 401(k), IRA, Bank Account, etc.]
- **Account Number** (Last 4 Digits): ____________________
- **Institution/Organization Name**: ____________________
- **Account Title:** [Individual Account, Joint Account, etc.]
- **Current Value of Account**: $ ____________________

2. Primary Beneficiary(ies)

I hereby designate the following individual(s) as the primary beneficiary(ies) to receive the assets of the above account(s) upon my death:

Primary Beneficiary 1:

- Full Legal Name: ____________________
- Address: ____________________
- Phone Number: ____________________

- Relationship to Account Holder: ____________________
- Percentage of Account Value: ____________________

Primary Beneficiary 2 (if applicable):

- Full Legal Name: ______________________________
- Address: ______________________________
- Phone Number: ______________________________
- Relationship to Account Holder: ____________________
- Percentage of Account Value: ____________________

Primary Beneficiary 3 (if applicable):

- Full Legal Name: ______________________________
- Address: ______________________________
- Phone Number: ______________________________
- Relationship to Account Holder: ____________________
- Percentage of Account Value: ____________________
- (Add additional beneficiaries as needed)

3. Contingent Beneficiary(ies)

If any primary beneficiary predeceases me, or is otherwise unable to receive their share of the account(s), I hereby designate the following individual(s) as contingent beneficiary(ies) to receive the assets of the above account(s):

Contingent Beneficiary 1:

- Full Legal Name: ______________________________
- Address: ______________________________
- Phone Number: ______________________________

- Relationship to Account Holder: ______________________
- Percentage of Account Value: ______________________

Contingent Beneficiary 2 (if applicable):

- Full Legal Name: ______________________________
- Address: ______________________________
- Phone Number: ______________________________
- Relationship to Account Holder: ______________________
- Percentage of Account Value: ______________________

Contingent Beneficiary 3 (if applicable):

- Full Legal Name: ______________________________
- Address: ______________________________
- Phone Number: ______________________________
- Relationship to Account Holder: ______________________
- Percentage of Account Value: ______________________
- (Add additional contingent beneficiaries as needed)

4. Distribution of Assets

The distribution of assets is as follows:

- The account(s) shall be distributed to the primary beneficiaries in the proportions specified above. If a primary beneficiary predeceases me, their share shall pass to their descendants, per stirpes.
- If all primary beneficiaries predecease me, the contingent beneficiaries shall receive the account(s) in the proportions specified above.

Contingent Instructions: In the event that no primary or contingent beneficiary survives me, the assets of the account(s) shall be distributed to my estate, to be handled according to the terms of my Will or applicable estate law.

5. Rights of the Beneficiary

The designated beneficiary(ies) shall have the right to claim the assets of the account(s) upon my death, subject to the terms and conditions of this Beneficiary Designation Form. The beneficiary(ies) shall be entitled to receive their designated share of the account(s) in accordance with the instructions outlined above.

6. Revocation of Previous Beneficiary Designations

I hereby revoke any and all previous beneficiary designations made by me for the above account(s), including those made in any prior forms, wills, or other documents, and this document supersedes all previous beneficiary designations.

7. Signature and Acknowledgment

By signing below, I affirm that I am the account holder and that I am executing this Beneficiary Designation Form voluntarily and with full understanding of its terms. I understand that this form shall control the distribution of the assets of the account(s) upon my death.

Account Holder's Signature: ____________________________

Date: ____________________________

8. Witness (Optional)

This form has been signed by the account holder in my presence. I hereby affirm that the account holder appeared to be of sound mind and was not under duress when signing this form.

Witness 1's Signature: ____________________________

Date: ______________________________

9. Notary Public (Optional, if required by institution)

State of ____________________ [State]

County of ___________________ [County]

On this _______ [Date], before me, a Notary Public, personally appeared [Account Holder's Full Name], known to me or provided identification, and acknowledged that they executed the same for the purposes therein contained.

Notary's Signature: ______________________________

Testamentary Trust Clause

A Testamentary Trust Clause is a provision in a will that creates a trust upon the testator's passing. It is often used to ensure structured asset distribution for minor children or dependents who may not be financially responsible at the time of inheritance.

Why Use a Testamentary Trust Clause?

This clause provides important benefits:

- **Delays Inheritance Until Maturity:** Ensures children receive funds only when they are old enough to manage them responsibly.
- **Controls Asset Distribution:** Prevents irresponsible spending by setting rules on when and how funds are accessed.
- **Appoints a Trustee for Management:** Assigns a reliable individual or institution to oversee the trust.
- **Ensures Financial Security:** Provides structured financial support for education, healthcare, and living expenses.

When Should You Include a Testamentary Trust Clause?

- **Children or dependents** may need financial management until they reach adulthood.
- **Specific conditions** should be met before heirs receive inheritance (e.g., age 25 or completion of education).
- **Avoiding lump-sum distributions** is preferred to prevent financial mismanagement.

How to Set Up and Use a Testamentary Trust Clause?

1. **Define Trust Terms:**
    - Establish the age or conditions under which beneficiaries can receive funds.
    - Specify how assets will be used before full distribution (e.g., education, healthcare).
2. **Appoint a Trustee:**
    - Choose a responsible individual or institution to manage trust assets.
3. **Draft the Clause in the Will:**
    - Work with an estate attorney to legally outline trust provisions in the will.
4. **Ensure Legal Compliance:**
    - Verify state-specific requirements for trust validity.
5. **Update as Needed:**
    - Adjust terms based on family needs or changing financial goals.

A Testamentary Trust Clause provides structured inheritance management, ensuring heirs receive financial support in a controlled manner. Proper planning prevents premature asset distribution while securing long-term financial stability for beneficiaries.

Testamentary Trust Clause

This TESTAMENTARY TRUST CLAUSE is made this _______ (Date), as part of my Last Will and Testament, by and between:

Testator:

- Full Legal Name: ________________________________
- Address: ________________________________
- Phone Number: ________________________________
- Email Address (optional): ________________________________

1. Establishment of Trust

Upon my death, I hereby establish a testamentary trust (the "Trust") under the terms outlined below. The Trust shall be funded with the assets of my estate as specified in my Last Will and Testament. The primary purpose of the Trust is to provide for the care, support, and maintenance of my designated beneficiary(ies) in accordance with my wishes.

2. Appointment of Trustee

I appoint ________________ [Trustee's Full Name], residing at ____________________________ [Trustee's Address], as the Trustee of this Trust. If __________________ [Trustee's Full Name] is unable or unwilling to serve, I appoint ________________ [Alternate Trustee's Full Name] as the Successor Trustee.The Trustee shall have the responsibility to manage and distribute the Trust assets in accordance with the terms of this Trust and the needs of the designated beneficiary(ies).

3. Beneficiary(ies)

The primary beneficiary(ies) of this Trust are as follows:

Primary Beneficiary 1:

- Full Legal Name: ______________________________
- Relationship to Testator: ______________________
- Percentage of Trust: ______________________

Primary Beneficiary 2:

- Full Legal Name: ______________________________
- Relationship to Testator: ______________________
- Percentage of Trust: ______________________

In the event that a primary beneficiary predeceases me, their share shall pass to their descendants, per stirpes, or as otherwise provided in my Last Will and Testament.

4. Trust Assets and Funding

The assets of this Trust shall consist of the following:

- Real Property: [Description of Real Property, if applicable]
- Financial Accounts: [Description of Financial Accounts, such as bank accounts, securities, etc.]
- Personal Property: [Description of Personal Property, such as valuable items, family heirlooms, etc.]

The Trustee shall have full discretion to manage, invest, and distribute these assets as necessary for the benefit of the beneficiaries.

5. Distribution of Trust Assets

The Trustee shall distribute the assets of the Trust in accordance with the following terms:

Distribution for Beneficiary(ies) during their Lifetime:

The Trustee shall distribute the Trust income and principal to the beneficiary(ies) in the following manner:

- [Percentage or amount] for the support and maintenance of the beneficiary(ies).
- Distributions shall be made on an [annual/quarterly/monthly] basis, as needed for the beneficiary(ies)'s health, education, maintenance, or support.

Final Distribution Upon the Death of the Beneficiary(ies):

Upon the death of the beneficiary(ies), the remaining assets in the Trust shall be distributed as follows:

- To [Full Legal Name of Secondary Beneficiary] [Relationship to Testator], in equal shares or as otherwise directed in my Will.

6. Powers of the Trustee

The Trustee shall have the following powers to manage the Trust assets:

- To sell, invest, and reinvest Trust assets in any lawful investment, including real estate, stocks, bonds, and mutual funds.
- To distribute income and principal to the beneficiary(ies) as needed for their support and well-being.
- To make decisions regarding the health, education, and support of the beneficiary(ies) in accordance with their best interests.
- To employ accountants, financial advisors, and attorneys as necessary for the administration of the Trust.

7. Successor Trustee

If the Trustee is unable or unwilling to serve, the Successor Trustee, ________________ [Successor Trustee's Full Name], shall take over the responsibilities of managing the Trust. If no Successor Trustee is named or if the

Successor Trustee is unable to serve, I appoint [Alternate Successor Trustee's Full Name] as the next Successor Trustee.

8. Trust Termination

This Trust shall terminate when all assets have been distributed to the beneficiaries, or upon the death of the last surviving beneficiary. Upon termination of the Trust, any remaining assets shall be distributed as follows:

- To _________________ [Alternate Beneficiary's Full Name] or to a charitable organization as designated in this Trust or in my Will.

9. Trustee's Compensation

The Trustee shall be entitled to reasonable compensation for their services in managing the Trust. If the Trustee is a family member or friend, they may serve without compensation, unless otherwise agreed upon.

10. No Contest Clause

If any beneficiary challenges the validity of this Trust or contests any of its provisions, they shall forfeit their share of the Trust assets.

11. Governing Law

This Trust shall be governed by and construed in accordance with the laws of the State of ___________ [State], and any disputes arising under this Trust shall be resolved in the courts of ____________ [County], ____________ [State].

12. Miscellaneous Provisions

- **Spendthrift Clause:** The Trust assets shall not be subject to the claims of creditors or other third parties.
- **Modification or Amendment:** This Trust may be modified or amended by the Grantor at any time during their lifetime, provided that the amendment is executed in writing and signed by the Grantor.

Signatures and Execution

Testator's Signature: ______________________________

Date: ______________________________

Trustee's Signature: ______________________________

Date: ______________________________

Witnesses (if required)

Witness 1's Signature: ______________________________

Date: ______________________________

Witness 2's Signature: ______________________________

Date: ______________________________

Notary Public (if required)

State of [State]

County of [County]

On this __________ [Date], before me, a Notary Public, personally appeared __________________ [Grantor's Full Name], known to me or provided identification, and acknowledged that they executed this document for the purposes therein contained.

Notary's Signature: ____________________________

Date: ____________________________

Special Needs Trust

A Special Needs Trust (SNT) is a legal arrangement designed to provide financial support for a disabled individual without jeopardizing their eligibility for government benefits such as Medicaid or Supplemental Security Income (SSI). It ensures funds are available for enhanced care, quality of life, and future expenses, while maintaining access to essential assistance programs.

Why Use a Special Needs Trust?

Creating an SNT offers several key benefits:

- **Preserves Government Aid Eligibility:** Assets placed in the trust are not counted for benefit qualification.
- **Ensures Financial Security:** Provides funds for housing, medical care, transportation, education, and other needs.
- **Protects Against Mismanagement:** A trustee oversees the funds, preventing financial exploitation.
- **Allows Flexibility for Expenses:** Covers non-covered essentials such as entertainment, therapy, and personal services.

When Should You Set Up a Special Needs Trust?

- **Planning for long-term care** and ongoing expenses.
- **Receiving an inheritance or financial settlement** that could affect benefit eligibility.
- **Ensuring structured financial management** to prevent fund misuse or depletion.

How to Set Up and Use a Special Needs Trust

1. **Select the Type of SNT:**
    - **First-Party SNT:** Created using the beneficiary's own funds (inheritance, lawsuit settlement, etc.).
    - **Third-Party SNT:** Funded by a parent, guardian, or other family members without affecting the beneficiary's assets.
    - **Pooled SNT:** Managed by a nonprofit, combining funds from multiple beneficiaries while maintaining individual accounts.
2. **Appoint a Trustee:**
    - Choose a reliable individual, financial institution, or nonprofit to manage funds and distributions responsibly.
3. **Define Trust Terms:**
    - Specify allowable expenses such as medical treatments, personal care, education, and leisure activities.
4. **Fund the Trust:**
    - Transfer assets, investments, or life insurance benefits into the trust.
5. **Ensure Legal Compliance:**
    - Work with an estate planning attorney to structure the trust properly and adhere to benefit regulations.
6. **Review and Adjust as Needed:**
    - Update the trust based on financial changes, legal developments, or evolving beneficiary needs.

A Special Needs Trust secures a dependent's financial future while maintaining government benefits. Proper planning prevents asset-related complications and ensures long-term stability and well-being for individuals with disabilities.

Special Needs Trust

This SPECIAL NEEDS TRUST (the "Trust") is made on this _______ (Date), by and between:

Grantor (Settlor):

- Full Legal Name: ______________________________
- Address: ______________________________
- Phone Number: ______________________________
- Email Address (optional): ______________________________

Trustee (the individual or institution managing the Trust):

- Full Legal Name: ______________________________
- Address: ______________________________
- Phone Number: ______________________________
- Email Address (optional): ______________________________

Beneficiary (the individual with special needs):

- Full Legal Name: ______________________________
- Address: ______________________________
- Phone Number: ______________________________
- Date of Birth: ______________________________

1. Declaration of Trust

The Grantor, [Grantor's Full Name], hereby establishes this Special Needs Trust for the benefit of [Beneficiary's Full Name], who has been diagnosed with [Brief

Description of Disability or Special Need]. The primary purpose of this Trust is to provide supplemental financial support for the Beneficiary while maintaining their eligibility for government assistance programs such as Medicaid, Supplemental Security Income (SSI), or other benefits.

2. Appointment of Trustee

I hereby appoint ____________________ [Trustee's Full Name] as the Trustee of this Special Needs Trust. If ____________________ [Trustee's Full Name] is unable or unwilling to serve as Trustee, I appoint ____________________ [Alternate Trustee's Full Name] as Successor Trustee.

3. Funding of the Trust

The Trust shall be funded by assets provided by the Grantor, including but not limited to cash, investments, real property, or any other assets of value. The assets held in the Trust will be used solely for the benefit of the Beneficiary, as described in the terms of this Agreement.

Initial Funding: The Trust is funded with the following assets:

- Cash: $____________________
- Real Property: ______________________________________ [Description of Property]
- Investments: ______________________________________ [List of Investments and Value]
- Personal Property: ______________________________________ [List of Property]

4. Trustee's Powers and Responsibilities

The Trustee shall have the following powers and responsibilities, which may be exercised in a manner that best serves the interests of the Beneficiary:

- To manage, invest, and reinvest the assets of the Trust in a manner that ensures its continued growth and preservation for the Beneficiary's benefit.
- To pay for the Beneficiary's supplemental care and needs, including housing, medical care, educational expenses, transportation, and recreational activities, without jeopardizing the Beneficiary's eligibility for government assistance.
- To purchase insurance, if needed, to protect the Trust's assets or the Beneficiary's health and well-being.
- To make distributions of the Trust's income and principal for the Beneficiary's care, well-being, and quality of life, subject to the limitations set forth in this Agreement.
- To employ attorneys, accountants, financial advisors, and other professionals as necessary for the management of the Trust.

5. Supplemental Support for the Beneficiary

The Trust is intended to supplement, not replace, government benefits to which the

Beneficiary is entitled. Therefore, the Trustee shall not make any distributions that would disqualify the Beneficiary from receiving public benefits, including SSI, Medicaid, or any other federal, state, or local assistance programs.

Permissible Expenses: The Trustee may make distributions for the following purposes:

- Medical and dental expenses not covered by insurance or public programs.
- Education and vocational training expenses.
- Clothing, transportation, and recreational activities.
- Social and cultural experiences that improve the quality of life.
- Special equipment or services, including assistive devices or therapy.

Prohibited Expenses: The Trustee shall not make distributions for:

- Basic living expenses, including food, shelter, or utilities, if such distributions would affect the Beneficiary's eligibility for government assistance.

6. Trustee's Discretion in Making Distributions

The Trustee shall have full discretion to make distributions from the Trust based on the needs of the Beneficiary, including but not limited to the needs outlined above. The Trustee is encouraged to make decisions in the best interests of the Beneficiary, ensuring that distributions are used to enhance the Beneficiary's quality of life without disqualifying them from government assistance.

7. Termination of the Trust

The Trust shall terminate upon the death of the Beneficiary or when the Trust's assets have been fully expended, whichever comes first. Upon termination, any remaining assets in the

Trust shall be distributed as follows:

- Remaining Assets: If there are any remaining funds in the Trust after the
- Beneficiary's death, they shall be distributed to [Alternate Beneficiary's Full Name] or to [Charitable Organization Name], as specified by the Grantor.
- Special Needs Consideration: If the Beneficiary has surviving descendants who may benefit from the remaining assets, the Trustee may choose to distribute the funds in a way that continues to benefit the family without violating applicable laws regarding public benefits.

8. Trust Duration and Modification

This Trust shall remain in effect during the lifetime of the Beneficiary and shall be modified only under the following circumstances:

- The Trustee may modify the terms of this Trust with the written consent of the Beneficiary (if capable) and the Grantor, or in the case of incapacity, the Successor Trustee.
- If there are changes to the Beneficiary's needs, the Trustee may amend the Trust to reflect these changes, provided that such modifications do not jeopardize the Beneficiary's eligibility for public assistance.

9. Trustee's Compensation

The Trustee shall be entitled to reasonable compensation for managing the Trust, which shall be determined by the prevailing rate for professional trustees or as agreed upon by the Grantor and Trustee. If the Trustee is a family member or a friend, the Trustee may serve without compensation unless otherwise agreed.

10. Trust Accounting and Reporting

The Trustee shall provide an annual accounting of the Trust's assets, income, and distributions to the Beneficiary or the Beneficiary's legal representative. The Trustee shall also provide a copy of the accounting to any interested parties upon request.

11. Governing Law

This Trust shall be governed by the laws of the State of [State], and any disputes regarding the interpretation or administration of the Trust shall be subject to the jurisdiction of the courts in ____________ [County], ___________ [State].

12. Miscellaneous Provisions

- **Spendthrift Clause**: The assets of the Trust shall not be subject to the claims of creditors of the Beneficiary.

- **No Contest Clause**: If any beneficiary contests the validity of this Trust or attempts to challenge its terms, they shall forfeit any share of the Trust assets.

Signatures and Execution

Grantor's Signature: ____________________________

Date: ____________________________

Trustee's Signature: ____________________________

Date: ____________________________

Witnesses (if applicable)

Witness 1's Signature: ____________________________

Date: ____________________________

Witness 2's Signature: ____________________________

Date: ____________________________

Notary Public (if required)

State of [State]

County of [County]

On this _________ [Date], before me, a Notary Public, personally appeared _______________ [Grantor's Full Name] and __________________ [Trustee's Full

Name], known to me or provided identification, and acknowledged that they executed the same for the purposes therein contained.

Notary's Signature: ______________________________

Date: ______________________________

Conclusion

As we finish our look at living trusts and estate planning, let's think about what we've learned together. Estate planning isn't just for those with abundant resources; it's a vital tool for everyone who wishes to take control of their financial legacy. Understanding the basics of living trusts unlocks greater control over your financial future, allowing you to make informed and confident decisions. Whether you're someone meticulously planning your estate or someone seeking affordable options to secure your assets for loved ones, knowledge is indeed power.

Imagine the freedom that comes from understanding the complexities of estate planning. The moment you grasp these vital concepts, the once-daunting process turns into a manageable task that feels both achievable and rewarding. Remember, it's not about memorizing every legal term but truly understanding how each aspect benefits you and aligns with your vision for the future. With clarity, you can craft a plan that mirrors your personal aspirations and secures the well-being of those you hold dear.

Simplicity is key. No one enjoys wading through endless jargon, especially when considering something as important as your estate. That's why we've focused on breaking down these concepts into digestible pieces, making them not only understandable but also actionable. When you simplify the pathway, planning becomes less of a chore and more of a strategic act of caregiving for your family. It's about creating space for your loved ones to thrive without being burdened by unnecessary complexity.

Proactive planning cannot be underestimated. It lays the foundation for a seamless transition of assets and shields your family from potential conflicts after you're gone. By setting clear intentions and taking initiatives today, you ensure peace of mind tomorrow. Imagine your family gathered together, focused not on disputes or confusion, but on celebrating the memories and legacy you've left behind. This foresight offers them emotional space, away from the stress of unresolved matters, allowing them to support each other during challenging times.

Communication remains the bedrock upon which successful estate planning stands. Encouraging open dialogues within your family about estate intentions fosters transparency, eliminates guesswork, and cultivates trust. It's important for every member of the family to understand your wishes and the responsibilities they might hold. Such openness transforms what could be a source of tension into an opportunity for unity and collective understanding. It is through these meaningful conversations that families grow closer, enabling them to honor your wishes with confidence and mutual respect.

Encouraging open conversations and active engagement in estate planning ensures that you're not only organizing your assets but also supporting and preparing your loved ones for the future. This preparation ensures they're ready to handle challenges with grace and dedication, grounded in the knowledge that they're fulfilling your carefully considered wishes.

Let us also acknowledge the importance of accessibility. Many shy away from estate planning due to perceived inaccessibility or fear of exorbitant costs. However, there are numerous ways to navigate these concerns without sacrificing quality or peace of mind. Affordable solutions exist, offering the guidance needed without overwhelming financial commitment. Exploring these routes removes barriers and empowers everyone to undertake estate planning as an essential component of responsible financial stewardship.

In essence, concluding this book is not the end of your learning journey. Instead, it is an invitation to continue engaging with these topics as part of your life. Remember, your estate plan is not static. It should evolve with changes in your life circumstances and aspirations. Revisiting your strategies ensures they remain aligned with your current desires and legislative landscapes.

As you walk away from these pages, carry forward the spirit of empowerment, simplicity, and active engagement we've embraced throughout. Empowerment, because you now hold the keys to shaping your financial destiny. Simplicity, because you see through the fog of complexity to the clear path ahead. Engagement, because every conversation you start brings your dreams for tomorrow closer to reality.

May your newfound understanding inspire confidence and lead you to not only secure your present but also establish a meaningful legacy for the future. Let this be your call to action, to forge plans that genuinely mirror your hopes and serve as guiding lights for generations to come.

Protect Your Legacy Today with 14 FREE Living Trust Templates!

Take the next step in securing your family's future with **14 FREE Living Trust templates** from *The Beginner's Guide to Living Trusts*. These essential documents are designed to save you time, money, and the hassle of hiring expensive lawyers.

What You'll Get:

- **Durable Power of Attorney** – Appoint someone to manage your finances if you're unable.
- **Pour-Over Will** – Ensure any assets not included in your trust are transferred automatically.
- **Advanced Health Care Directive** – Specify your medical treatment preferences in case you're unable to communicate.
- **Pet Trust Template** – Protect your beloved pets with clear instructions for their care.
- **And More** – All the essential documents you need to create your trust with ease.

Why Choose These Templates?

- **Easy-to-use**: Clear, step-by-step instructions guide you through the process.
- **Cost-effective**: Skip expensive lawyer fees and handle your estate planning on your own.
- **Comprehensive**: Get everything you need to protect your family and assets.

Start planning your legacy today with the peace of mind knowing your loved ones will be taken care of.

Get your 14 FREE Living Trust templates that you can start using immediately!

End of Life Planner that Includes A Complete Record of My Accounts, Heirlooms and More

References

Absolute Law Group. (2024, June 10). Updating your estate plan after major life changes. Absolute Law Group. https://www.absolutelawgroup.com/post/updating-your-estate-plan-after-major-life-changes

Busch, D. (2024, October 29). Types of trusts and their uses: A comprehensive guide. Elayne.com. https://www.elayne.com/resources/types-of-trusts-and-their-uses-a-comprehensive-guide

Choosing a health care proxy. (2022, October 31). National Institute on Aging. https://www.nia.nih.gov/health/advance-care-planning/choosing-health-care-proxy

Dolyna, L. (2025, March 1). Which trust expenses are really tax deductable? - avoid this mistake + faqs. Tax Shark. https://taxsharkinc.com/which-trust-expenses-are-tax-deductable/

Five things you didn't know about financial power of attorney. (n.d.). Trust & Will. https://trustandwill.com/learn/financial-power-of-attorney

Haughton, D. (2025, March 5). Estate planning in the digital age: Why digital assets are a critical part and how to help clients address them. Nerd's Eye View | Kitces.com. https://www.kitces.com/blog/estate-planning-digital-assets-documentation-financial-holdings-inventory-cryptocurrency-investment-online/

Hoonings, V. (2025a, April 26). Comparing DIY estate planning software: Features and costs. Wills.com. https://learning-center.wills.com/comparing-diy-estate-planning-software-features-costs/

Hoonings, V. (2025b, April 26). Comparing DIY estate planning software: Features and costs. Wills.com. https://learning-center.wills.com/comparing-diy-estate-planning-software-features-costs/

How to fund a trust: Key steps and what to consider. (2025, April 28). Wealth.com. https://www.wealth.com/resources/estate-planning/how-to-fund-a-trust-key-steps-and-what-to-consider/

How to select the ideal trustee for your trust: Key characteristics and skill traits. (n.d.). Eannarinolaw.com. https://eannarinolaw.com/selecting-a-trustee/

Klieger, M. (n.d.). Estate planning for minors: Secure guardianship and trusts. Matthew Klieger. https://matthewklieger.com/estate-planning-minors-guardianship-trusts/

Law Librarianship Editorial. (2024, May 11). Understanding probate fees and costs: A comprehensive guide. https://lawlibrarianship.com/probate-fees-and-costs/

Legal update | understanding the 2026 changes to the estate, gift, and generation-skipping tax exemptions. (2024, June 13). Huschblackwell.com . https://www.huschblackwell.com/newsandinsights/understanding-the-2026-changes-to-the-estate-gift-and-generation-skipping-tax-exemptions

Our Attorney. (2024, October 18). Strategies for Probate Avoidance in Estate Planning. Guiding Legal Counsel. https://guidingcounsel.com/strategies-for-probate-avoidance-in-estate-planning/

Parker, M. (2024, October 21). Which assets should I include in my trust? Estate and Trust Lawyer. https://www.estateandtrustlawyer.com/which-assets-should-i-include-in-my-trust/

Parker, M. (2025, March 12). My guide to trust amendments: How to update my living trust understanding . Estate and Trust Lawyer. https://www.estateandtrustlawyer.com/my-guide-to-trust-amendments-how-to-update-my-living-trust-understanding/

Rahn, S. (2020, November). What is an appointment of a successor trustee? Rmolawyers.com. https://rmolawyers.com/blog/what-is-appointment-of-successor-trustee/

Tamplin, T. (2025, April 17). Tax-Efficient gifting strategies | definitions and examples. Finance Strategists. https://www.financestrategists.com/tax/tax-planning/tax-efficient-gifting-strategies/

Team, T. G. (2022, April 16). Breaking down the different parts of a trust. Gentreo. https://www.gentreo.com/breaking-down-the-different-parts-of-a-trust

Ten key components of a comprehensive estate plan. (n.d.). Calkins Law Firm. https://calkinslawfirm.com/10-key-components-of-a-comprehensive-estate-plan/

Trustee reporting and record-keeping requirements. (n.d.). Attorney Aaron Hall. https://aaronhall.com/trustee-reporting-and-record-keeping-requirements/

Trusts and estates: Six fiduciary duties every trustee must know . (n.d.). Attorney Aaron Hall. https://aaronhall.com/trusts-and-estates-6-fiduciary-duties-every-trustee-must-know/

Understanding the revocation of trust in estate planning. (2023, July 3). The Law Offices of James L. Arrasmith. https://www.jlegal.org/blog/understanding-the-revocation-of-trust-in-estate-planning/

www.ingramcontent.com/pod-product-compliance
Lightning Source LLC
LaVergne TN
LVHW021744071126
851857LV00039B/698
* 9 7 8 1 9 6 6 4 8 9 2 1 4 *